PIE & WHISKEY

EDITED BY
KATE LEBO
& SAMUEL LIGON

PIE
&
WHISKEY

WRITERS UNDER THE INFLUENCE
OF BUTTER &
BOOZE

SASQUATCH BOOKS
SEATTLE

Printed in Canada | Published by Sasquatch Books

21 20 19 18 17   9 8 7 6 5 4 3 2 1

Library of Congress Cataloging-in-Publication Data is available.

ISBN: 978-1-63217-112-2

Sasquatch Books | 1904 Third Avenue, Suite 710, Seattle, WA 98101
(206) 467-4300 | www.sasquatchbooks.com | custserv@sasquatchbooks.com

EDITOR: GARY LUKE | PRODUCTION EDITOR: BRIDGET SWEET
ILLUSTRATIONS: MIKE BAEHR | DESIGN: TONY ONG
COPYEDITOR: MICHELLE HOPE ANDERSON
AUTHOR PHOTO: ADRIANA JANOVICH

TO PIE EATERS AND WHISKEY DRINKERS EVERYWHERE

CONTENTS

3

4

5

6

7

8

DEAR READER

Pie & Whiskey started in 2012 as a reading in Spokane, Washington. The idea was to serve good pie, good whiskey, and good writers reading prose or poetry about pie and whiskey. We thought there was something right about the combination—pie in your left hand, whiskey in your right. We thought there was something weirdly American about it, too—Saturday night debauch meets Sunday morning brunch. Cowboys don't walk into saloons and order gin. We don't say, "American as motherhood and apple cake."

That first year, we lined up twelve writers to read for five minutes each, sent them a pie prompt and a whiskey prompt to inspire new work, and told them the whole thing was low stakes. Get Lit!, Spokane's literary festival, agreed to host us at the Spokane Woman's Club. We asked Don Poffenroth, of Dry Fly Distilling, to donate the whiskey. He gave us six fifths, which we thought would be plenty. We baked ten pies and hoped fifty people would come, a pretty good audience for a reading.

The night of the show, over three hundred people piled into the Woman's Club or waited in line outside. Thirty minutes after we opened the doors, we ran out of pie. Five minutes after that, we ran out of whiskey. People with pie and whiskey and people without pie and whiskey sat in pews, at banquet tables, on the stage, on the floor. People stood between the chairs and leaned on the walls. People were everywhere.

We worried that we wouldn't be able to hold the room. We worried that the people who hadn't been served would leave.

Then Steve Almond, our first reader, shouted for everyone to please shut up. People drank their whiskey and ate their pie quietly, then not so quietly because Steve was so funny. Eleven more writers read that night. Nobody left.

We did it again the next year, and four hundred people showed up. We poured two cases of whiskey, donated by Don and Dry Fly, and baked twenty pies.

We ran out of everything again, but everyone got served—a phenomenon Gary Copeland Lilley referred to in year three as "some loaves-and-fishes shit."

We'd said from the beginning that Pie & Whiskey should be about the pie, the whiskey, and the reading—in that order. Whiskey alone is no different from any gathering of writers. Pie alone is a family affair. And most readings put people to sleep. At Pie & Whiskey, there is no sleeping. It's not a family affair, either, or a drunken affair. The readings are by adults, for adults, but no one gets too out of hand. People have a good time with friends and strangers, and they let their guard down.

We think Pie & Whiskey works because it fulfills a craving for community and connection in a time when community is too often a Facebook feed and connection is a targeted ad. By serving up great writing and sugary, boozy treats, we create a social space where the audience engages in a kind of conspiracy with the writers, the writers are also audience members, and the writers and the audience feed off each other, all of us eating homemade pie and drinking good, local whiskey, with no kids in the place. This night is for adults only, which means we can be entirely adolescent as we read and listen to stories about bad breakups and bad sex and good sex and bad drugs and good drugs and church and politics and whiskey and pie and everything else that happens after the kiddies go to bed. The writers always deliver at this event—maybe because the audience is right there with them, rooting for the readings, urging them to be funny, outrageous, and true.

But the power is not just in the air of the moment. You can feel it on the page, too, when you read the Pie & Whiskey zines we hand-bind for each reading. Because the writing prompts seem so unserious, there's a sense of play in the pieces that's all the more exciting because the writers are so good. We hope this anthology captures that pleasure and ache, that Pie-&-Whiskey spirit of sweetness tinged with something sharp.

The majority of these pieces were written for live Pie & Whiskey readings in either Spokane, Washington, or Missoula, Montana, but the long pieces—one to anchor each of eight sections—are new. You'll find recipes for pie inspired by these new pieces, and whiskey cocktails, too, plus instructions for how to throw your own Pie & Whiskey reading.

So bake some pies, pour some drinks, and enjoy these meditations on butter and booze. As the Irish say, "What butter and whiskey won't cure, there is no cure for."

Yours in sweet corruption,

KATE LEBO & SAM LIGON
Spokane, Washington
November 15, 2016

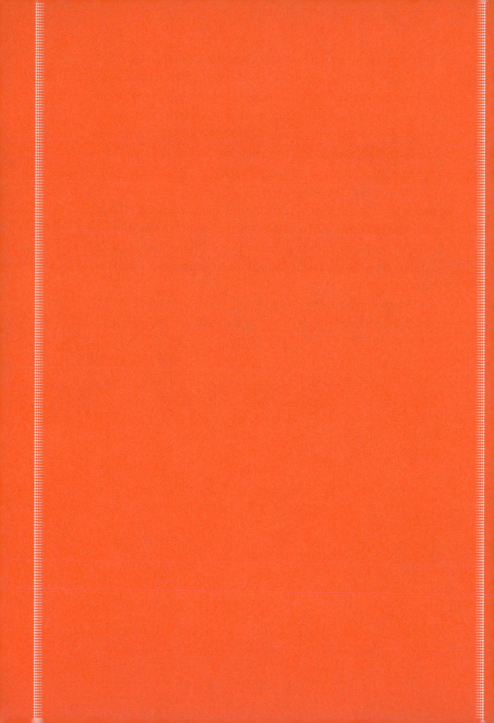

I

Pie is the food of the heroic.
No pie-eating people can ever be
permanently vanquished.

—*NEW YORK TIMES*, MAY 3, 1902

PIE <u>AND</u> WHISKEY

ROBERT WRIGLEY

There's apple and peach, pecan and cherry,
lemon meringue, and tart strawberry.
There's bourbon, Canadian, Scotch, and rye,
plus key lime, blackberry, and shoofly pie.
Ten High, rotgut, Jack, and Jim Beam,
mincemeat, rhubarb, and banana cream.
Raisin, Black Velvet, sour mash, and plum,
whisky or whiskey: it won't work with rum.
Pork pie and pumpkin, Maker's Mark and pot,
they're good with a little, better with a lot.
Kidney and apricot and old Wild Turkey,
and some abomination made with chunks of Tofurky.
There's Dickel and Knob Creek, chocolate and mud
(no Jägermeister, please; it's like VapoRub).
A friend says pie's love and cake is pure lust,
and it can't be a pie with a graham cracker crust.
He will not drink any whiskey but bourbon

and finds small-batch stuff effete and hipster urban.
Now me? I love chess pie with hot Irish coffee.
I love to dunk in that whiskeyey broth such toffee
as almost pulls my fillings loose,
with Midleton, Redbreast, or Old Blue Caboose.
O pie and whiskey, whiskey and pie,
Dalwhinnie and Oban and WhistlePig rye.
Cheese pie and hare pie (by that I mean rabbit:
though the other one's also a savory habit).
There's Basil Hayden's and blueberry cream,
and fandango boysenberry sweet cheese supreme.
Sazerac, sweet potato, Tullamore D.E.W.
the list goes on endlessly, I think, don't you?
But pie crust's like skin, both salt and sweety,
and the word *whiskey* derives from aqua vitae.
That's the water of life, friends, and it's fierce and strong,
and the crust makes pie perfect, if I'm not wrong.
So drink and eat and nibble such pastry
as you're lucky to come upon, and may it be tasty,
with Talisker, Jameson, and all fine pies' delight:
that all may drink, eat, and even more, tonight.

THE OLD TOWN

RACHEL TOOR

IT IS THE COCKTAIL of sorority girls, liquid license to let hands wander and mouths find their way, lubrication for the mating call of that sexually ambivalent herd: "I can't feel my face."

As a twentysomething I would have been embarrassed to order a 7 and 7; it seemed a bad cultural signifier, and I was concerned, then, with signifying. Now, though I cannot taste the difference between cheap liquor and more spendy brands, I will buy upscale whiskey in well-formed bottles and mix it with Diet 7Up. Into a fizzy glass I will plop four maraschino cherries and spoon in enough juice to make it sweeter than bad pie, and pink. I am, three decades later, finally secure enough to drink something pink.

Scotch and soda was what I drank then. I didn't like the color, didn't like the smell, didn't like the taste, but after college, when I worked in editorial at a publishing house that had, only a few years before I joined, celebrated its quincentenary, five hundred years of publishing Bibles and often dull monographs by dusty scholars, I drank Scotch. Days I read manuscripts on international telecommunications policy and the Masonic movement in western Massachusetts, and at night I went with production assistants and copywriters and publicists to the Old Town. They ordered pitchers. I drank Scotch because I couldn't abide the taste of beer and because Scotch seemed like a serious drink. It was important then to appear serious. I ordered it with soda because I liked the romance, liked saying scotchandsoda, liked how the bubbles tamed the bite.

The Old Town was just a bar we went to, a close enough walk from the office, dark not dingy. Maybe there was food and maybe the food was good; I could never afford to both eat and drink and so stuck with well Scotch because it felt more necessary. It was just the Old Town, with a long marble and mahogany bar, and high ceilings of hammered tin, which meant something to people who bought apartments in New York but were only words to me. The floor feels sticky in my memory. The narrowness made it overcrowded if you hadn't already snagged a booth. Our jobs let us off early enough to settle in before the slick-haired arbitrageurs and traders came wearing their improbable suits. In a few years they would be aping Michael Douglas playing Gordon Gekko quoting Sun Tzu. They would not know we had published a translation of *The Art of War*. We might brush against them at the Dublin House on the Upper West Side after a softball game in Central Park, or at Chumley's on a rare night downtown; maybe we'd all get postcard invites to parties at Area and the Palladium and Limelight, but we lived in a different city. They had money and youth, and we had youth and moral superiority.

When you're twenty-four years old and paying more than half your salary to rent what the building calls an apartment but is really a converted hotel room no bigger than an area rug, where, when you sit on the toilet, your knees touch the door, and the kitchen is a corner by the window with a mini fridge and a hot plate, and you spend your days editing manuscripts that become books only a handful of people will ever read, you need to believe in your moral superiority.

Unalienated labor, I called it, proud that my age exceeded my salary. I used possessives and plural pronouns with enthusiasm and returned the calls of "my" authors promptly, told them "we" were thrilled to be publishing their book. They would come to Manhattan from their small college towns, and I would take them to Keens Chophouse, with its collection of clay pipes and its men's club smell. They would order shad roe or calf's liver with onions, and I'd say to them when the waiter came around, "What would you like?" signaling that it was I who had the expense account, that I, with too-frizzy hair and street earrings and a Coach bag and desperate shoes, was to get the check. I didn't realize that these academic men were happy to be bought lunch.

Sometimes they'd ask me to dinner. I wouldn't say yes unless I'd already met and liked them, but often I liked them. And they liked me. I didn't know they experienced my wanting to publish their work and wanting them as interchangeable, that my eagerness made me attractive. I was the attentive audience, the ideal reader. For many of them, that was enough. More than enough.

They touched me on the arm, placed a hand on the small of my back as we entered the restaurant. On these nights they would tell me they were paying, and they'd take me to Café des Artistes or to the bar at the Essex House on Central Park South, which, if you looked at the sign from far enough away, seemed to read "EZ-SEX House." Close your eyes, one said, and I felt his hands just above my knees, where my short skirt couldn't reach. He cupped a pair of malachite earrings he'd brought back from South Africa. For you, he said. I finished my Scotch and soda and then, before I hailed a cab, let him kiss me in a dark doorway. You're married, I said, and he said, Yes, yes. And You. He said, You.

They went on to college presidencies and confirmation hearings and endowed professorships, these men. Now I hear them on NPR or see them quoted in the *New York Times*, remember how I served for them as a magnifying mirror, and blush at the power I once thought I had.

BLOODLINES

VIRGINIA REEVES

I HAVE NOT ALWAYS bled whiskey.

As an infant, it was blood, pure and expected. Prone to injury from the start, my new skin wore red lines.

"Do you have a cat?" people asked my mother. "A mean one?"

She answered with a shake of her head and no other explanation.

At five, my blood thinned, running from cuts with new speed. I bled fast and healed faster. At ten, it lightened in color, and my classmates watched in awe as I ran the blade of my very own pocketknife across my palm, light-pink water pouring forth, more the fluid of childbirth than veins, something to drink. When the bell rang at the end of recess, my hand was already healed, the knife back in my pocket, a secret my fellow students kept for me.

I couldn't tell the difference between attention out of love or fear, and so the playground tricks continued, a warmth in my belly from the wonderment in my peers' eyes.

Physical pain is something I've never felt. My mother calls this a curse, like my shifty blood.

Edward was the first to ask after the flavor. Never part of the circling pack, he lingered at edges, catching me after school late in my junior year of high school. We were in ceramics together. He'd watched me bleed on the wheel, a tool nicking the index finger of my left hand. By then, my blood was clear. It mixed with the water I sponged over the clay, everything muddy.

"Is it salty?" he asked.

"What?"

"Your blood."

I didn't know. I'd never brought a cut to my mouth to ease the pain. The taste of blood referenced in books—copper, iron, pennies, metal—was all invention to me, fantasy.

"Is yours?" I asked.

"Everyone's is."

I took the knife from my pocket and opened a line in my hand, the liquid glistening in the spring sun, rivulets pouring between the webbing of my fingers, dripping from my knuckles into the greening grass. I dipped a finger in. Edward, too.

"Not salty."

"No," he agreed. "But something strong."

We met after school again the next day, stealing away to a park, our backs to an old fir. He pulled reapportioned spice jars from his backpack, each full of liquid, masking tape covering the old labels, new names written in his blocky print. His parents had a well-stocked bar.

He held out an empty bottle and nodded toward my hand. I'd never collected my blood before. One cut filled the jar halfway; two topped it off.

Edward wrote *Mary* on the label, and then we started sampling, a sip of mine after each sip of the others.

He grew silly by the fourth, his words slurring slightly, a new brightness to his speech, more touch in his fingers. I didn't realize it was the alcohol that allowed him to kiss me, that drowned his nerves enough to make the move. It was my first kiss.

"You didn't get drunk," he said the next day.

Like pain and the salty taste of blood, drunkenness is another thing I'll never experience. We decided my blood was vodka, a young liquor, immature.

I don't blame Edward for telling, for the lines that formed at lunch, the requests for sips in the hall, the vessels brought in for weekend parties, the invitations. I was the most popular person, homecoming queen come senior year, prom queen as well. I spiked the punch, filled the flasks. I held no elected office and wasn't valedictorian, but my class demanded I make a speech at graduation. Edward wrote it for me. We'd become a couple by then, voted most likely to get married.

Add marriage to that list of things I'll never know—exploitation of my blood too tempting, too easy.

There was no need for me to go to college, but I did move away. I send my mother money but no news. I've not seen Edward for years.

I travel the West Coast, San Diego to the tiny village of Neah Bay, far at the tip of Washington. They don't know where the whiskey comes from, only that it's the most prized in the world. If something is good enough, it can quiet any question.

WHISKEY PIE

JESS WALTER

CHAPTER I | THE SPLIT

THEIR LAST KID WAS barely out the door when Ron and Leslie called it quits. No warning, no counseling, no trial separation—it was thirty years and straight to divorce. The news devastated the four adult Madden children, and what followed, their parents' blithe nonchalance, only made it worse. *It was time for a change,* Ron and Leslie said.

As if they were trading in a Subaru.

The Madden kids compared their parents' trite, coordinated responses at a coffee shop near their house, agitated hands working the paper cups of their lattes. Dean, the oldest at twenty-five, had just gotten engaged, under subtle but unending pressure from his girlfriend, Kirsten. He suggested it might have been nice for his parents to let him know, *I don't know—BEFORE I got engaged?*

The youngest, nineteen-year-old Gwen, had just left for college. *Oh my god, guys,* she said, *do you think this is MY fault?*

Yes, her siblings said.

Twenty-three-year-old Charlie and twenty-two-year-old Claire also responded in typical fashion, Claire collapsing into a lip-quivering, crying lump, the recently born-again Charlie resorting to the kind of language he rarely used: *This is such bull you-know-what.*

Ron and Leslie had married young and had four children in six years. Ron was the office manager for a residential developer that specialized in faux townhouses; Leslie stayed home. Theirs was such a rock-solid traditional marriage that divorce had never even occurred to the children. That sense of shock was phrased a hundred different ways but always led to the same question:

What happened?

Nothing happened, Ron and Leslie insisted. *It was just time.*

Increasingly frustrated, the kids chose emissaries—Dean to their dad, Claire to their mom—to deliver a unified message: *Give it one more try, if not for you, for us.*

Ron listened as he boxed up his socket set in his garage. He chose his words with great care, like a man searching for the right socket. *Dean, that is not . . . what either of us wants.*

Leslie was even more direct with Claire. She was packing for a three-week Central American singles cruise, during which she and the other passengers would do relief work with poor children before returning every night to the ship for salsa dancing on the lido deck.

Listen to me, honey, Leslie said. *I want to make sure you hear this. Your father and I are NEVER getting back together.*

Snot bubbles of grief shot forth from Claire.

Days later, when the Maddens' five-bedroom rancher on the backside of Spokane's South Hill went up for sale, the kids took turns calling one another, sputtering with disbelief. Where would they spend the holidays? What about the furniture in their old bedrooms? This wasn't just a house; their very childhood was on the market.

I'm still in college! Gwen said.

I imagine they're aware of that, Dean said.

Priced to move, the rancher sold in two weeks.

Then something happened that explained the divorce to the Madden kids: Ron announced he was moving in with a woman from the neighborhood, the Widow Cartwright.

Julie Cartwright had lost her husband ten years earlier in a car accident, leaving her, at the time, young, attractive, and alone. After a short mourning period that hardly seemed suitable to the power-walking moms in the neighborhood, the Widow Cartwright began wearing tight dresses and staying out late. Strange sedans and pickups showed up parked cockeyed in her driveway in the mornings. Then, five years ago, the Widow Cartwright gave birth to her only child (out of wedlock, the neighborhood power-walkers did not need to be reminded), a special-needs girl named Tami. The Widow Cartwright didn't venture out much and kept her drapes closed, so the exact nature of Tami's birth defects remained the topic of conjecture—some said she was blind and had stubbly arms, others said she actually had paddles for hands and no teeth.

Wait, Dean said. *Do you think our dad is that penguin freak's father?*

Gwen couldn't fathom it. *So you're telling me I have a penguin stepsister?*

Penguin HALF sister, said Dean.

Bullcrap! said Charlie.

Claire wept.

It makes sense, Dean said. *Mrs. Cartwright was a total WILF . . . Widow I'd like to—*

Yes, the others said. *We get it.*

In spite of the deep disapproval of his children, in October Ron moved in with the Widow Cartwright and their paddle-handed love child, Tami.

I am not commenting, said Leslie from the Mexican port town of Lázaro Cárdenas, where Claire reached her by phone.

What do you mean she wouldn't comment? Gwen asked.

Did she think it was a press conference? asked Dean.

Charlie's face burned. *Total bullcrap.*

Now you're just being crazy, Dean said to his brother.

Claire wept.

A few weeks after Ron moved in, the Widow Cartwright reached out to his children. Thanksgiving was coming in a couple of weeks, and Mrs. Cartwright—*Please, call me Julie*—suggested by mass e-mail that she and Ron have Thanksgiving at their house (*THEIR house!?*) Unfortunately, the widow Cartwright admitted, she wasn't the world's greatest cook (*Ha-ha,* she wrote, and *LOL* and a winking semicolon with a smiling parenthesis). So wouldn't it be fun to have . . . a potluck! Everyone could bring something. She and Ron would make a turkey, but the kids could bring the rest. Wasn't that a great way to get to know each other?

Un-stinking-believable, said Charlie.

The woman's a nutjob, Dean said. *Who invites people for Thanksgiving and makes THEM bring the food?*

And that wasn't the end of it. The Thanksgiving invitation was followed a day later with an addendum. Mrs. Cartwright had gone through a period of heavy drinking after the death of her husband and was a recovering alcoholic who hadn't touched a drop in five years. If it wasn't too much to ask, she inquired politely, could Ron's children please refrain from bringing any alcohol into her house?

Of course, the children wrote back, and *Certainly* and *You betcha* and *Can't wait.*

And that's how the adult children of Ron and Leslie Madden ended up preparing this menu for their first potluck Thanksgiving dinner with their new stepmom and their half sister:

Beer-braised beef skewers

Whiskey-stout yams
Margarita shrimp salad
Bourbon-basted brussels sprouts
Vodka-steamed green beans

And for dessert, devout Charlie's contribution, a chocolate pecan whiskey pie, a recipe that called for a quarter cup of Jack Daniel's— an amount the teetotaling Charlie ignored, pouring in *four cups* of whiskey, so that the pie never set, the pecans bobbing like flotsam, hunks of crust floating on the whiskey like moss on a stagnant pond.

CHAPTER 3 | COCKTAIL HOUR

Julie wanted a drink. Five years later, those four simple words, *I want a drink,* were still the most apt description for the complex web of feelings that overwhelmed her—anxiety, self-loathing, and deep sadness. After Michael died, her grief had been a vast expanse of sorrow she shrank to those four manageable words: *I want a drink.*

Today was so bad because she'd brought the anxiety on herself. What was she thinking, hosting Thanksgiving just weeks after Ron moved in? Maybe hopeful and stupid were the same thing.

I wish you hadn't asked them to bring their own food was all Ron said.

She'd thought a potluck would be fun.

Fun, Ron repeated flatly.

Children are adaptable and resourceful, Julie said. *Forgiving.*

Yeah, Ron answered. *Mine aren't.*

The four words broke into halves in her addled mind: *I want. A drink.* They climbed like musical scales: *I want a DRINK.* They swung open like a gate: *I want . . . a drink.*

There was a meeting in the basement of First Presbyterian; she could make it, but she might not be back before Ron's kids arrived. Great first impression: *Sorry I'm late. Had to run to an AA meeting.*

Julie looked over at Ron: sallow, weary, shadows beneath his deep-set eyes. He was a good man—loyal, kind—but he didn't handle conflict well (obviously, having lived in a dead marriage for so long). He slowly folded napkins at the dining room table. He hefted the silverware for each place setting as if the forks weighed thirty pounds. There were four bottles of sparkling cider in the center of the table; Julie had the urge to open one and pound it. Maybe she could get a carbonation buzz.

Ron looked up. *It's going to be fine, Julie,* he said, trying to be positive, his tone indicating that it would be fine in the same way climate change would be fine: one day they would both be dead and not have to be deal with it.

Julie knew she should call her sponsor, Sybil. Sybil was well aware of her situation; in fact, she had known Ron and Leslie for years. No-nonsense Sybil had served two tours in the army and now did physical therapy with veterans. She would walk Julie through the steps, through acceptance of her weakness and vulnerability, through her powerlessness, to peace and resolve. Julie went through each of the questions Sybil would ask: Have you had anything to drink? *No.* Are you in danger of drinking? *No.* Is there booze in the house? *No.* Do you feel like hurting herself? *No.* Then you're just anxious, Sybil would say. Everyone feels anxiety. But then Sybil would ask the most horrible question of all: *What are you making for Thanksgiving dinner?* As a sponsor Sybil was a real ballbuster. She was used to working with people who'd lost limbs in war, and she never let Julie get away with woe-is-me bullshit. She could imagine Sybil's gravelly voice. *Who the hell invites her boyfriend's kids over for POTLUCK Thanksgiving dinner! What were you thinking, Julie?* The words hung from the chandelier, rose from the table, fell from the sky: *I want a drink.*

Mama! Tami was awake.

Mama's coming, Julie said.

Mama now! Tami yelled.

Ron looked like a blood vessel might burst behind his temple. *I just wish you hadn't asked them to bring their own food.*

Julie turned back. *Yes, so you said.*

CHAPTER 4 | FIRST IMPRESSIONS

The Widow Cartwright's blond hair was graying, and she had little ravioli pockets beneath her eyes. She wore a blue flower-print dress that caused her arms to seem bony, while thickening her middle.

She looked, thought Gwen, like the substitute art teacher at a middle school.

She looked, thought Charlie, like a harlot.

She looked, thought Claire, like the kind of woman who might shoplift from a craft store.

She looked, thought Dean, sorta hot.

One by one, the Madden children came to the door, Mrs. Cartwright gaily accepting their booze-soaked entrées, exclaiming as she placed them on the elaborately set table. *Oh my.* And *This looks delicious.* And *What's in this sauce?*

Ginger, they said, and *Soy,* and *Lots of butter.*

Charlie left his whiskey pie in the car.

You don't want to bring it into the kitchen?

No, he said, *it needs to set. The cool air will be good for it.*

As they came in and set their food on the table, each kid looked around suspiciously. They examined Julie the same way, eyes moving up and down dismissively, those thick Madden brows climbing those long Madden foreheads, those long Madden faces saying, *You left our mother for THIS?* They stood awkwardly in a semicircle around Ron and Julie.

Where's Tami? Dean asked.

She takes a lot of naps, Ron said.

I'll bet, Dean said.

Dean seemed the friendliest, so she tried talking to him first. *And where is your fiancée . . . Is it Kirsten?*

Oh, we called off the engagement, Dean said. *You know, I guess the institution of marriage just seems like a sham to me now.*

They had all moved into the living room, Julie sitting, Ron standing behind her, dour as a nineteenth-century portrait. The three younger kids were on the couch, and Dean sprawled in Ron's favorite chair, the only piece of furniture they'd moved from his and Leslie's house.

Oh, Daddy, Claire said when she saw it. *Your chair!* She covered her mouth and began weeping.

The other three had bet on Claire's crying. Dean looked at his watch. *Anybody have nine minutes?*

Claire shot him a look.

Then it was quiet for six hours.

Dean didn't really call off his engagement, Claire said finally. *Kirsten just thought this would be too weird.*

Point Kirsten, Dean said.

After that it was quiet for eleven hours.

Come on, kids, Ron said helplessly. His children had been lying in wait for him to say something, and *Come on* was the best he could do? He'd selfishly flushed their whole world down the toilet to move in with this lunatic and her freak kid and then had the audacity to say, *Come on—*

They were eating the beef skewers as an appetizer.

This sauce is delicious, Mrs. Cartwright said. *What's in it?*

Beer, said Gwen. She glared from Mrs. Cartwright to her father and back. *There's alcohol in ALL the food. Is that a problem?*

For a moment it was quiet. *Excuse me,* Mrs. Cartwright said. She stood up and left the room.

No one could think of a thing to say.

Dean glared at Gwen, who simply shrugged, Gwenspeak for "Screw you." *I don't see what the big deal is. It all cooks off.*

They could hear the Widow Cartwright on the phone in the kitchen. *Yes*, she was saying, and *No*, and *I'll try.*

Jesus, Ron said to his kids.

But before he could imagine what might lie on the other side of that *Jesus*, there was a scream from down the hall. *Mama!* Their father snapped to attention and left the room to get Tami.

Dean sat up in his father's easy chair. This was about to get good.

CHAPTER 6 | DINNER

She didn't have flippers at all. In fact her arms and hands were perfectly formed. She wasn't blind and didn't have a duckbill or a tail or anything; she was just maybe a little developmentally delayed. So even though she was almost five, she was more like a big toddler, crooked smile on her face and a diaper underneath a short party dress. She ran into the room, clutching a stuffed hippo. She moved from Madden kid to Madden kid, facing them with the most expansive smile.

I Tami! she said.

Hi, Tami, Dean said.

I Tami!

Hi, Tami, Charlie said.

God, she was adorable. Also, she was black. Or mixed race, actually—obviously, since the Widow Cartwright was white: she had light-brown skin and short loose curls, lovely green eyes. *I Tami!* she said to Claire, and realizing she'd already introduced herself to this big person, she covered her eyes with her hands and said, *Oof.*

Claire began weeping.

Then Mrs. Cartwright came out of the kitchen, eyes red as if she'd also been crying, holding a plate of sliced wheat bread. *Let's eat,* she said. She set the bread down and fled into the kitchen again.

The kids moved uneasily to the dining room, sat as the vacant-eyed Ron secured Tami in the largest high chair any of them had ever seen.

Mrs. Cartwright swept back in from the kitchen with the turkey and a hastily prepared salad, little more than some violently torn iceberg lettuce. She settled in next to Ron. *Dig in,* she said, voice uneasy. She forced a smile as she passed each plate, but she eschewed the food Ron's children had brought and ate only the things from her own dry kitchen: turkey, wheat bread without butter, plain lettuce.

Charlie cleared his throat—*What about grace?* But Dean shot him a look. They ate quietly.

This turkey's delicious, Charlie said finally.

Thank you, Charlie, Mrs. Cartwright said.

Ron avoided his kids' boozy food, too, until Mrs. Cartwright saw what he was doing and nudged the bourbon-soaked brussels sprouts toward him. *Please, Ron.*

He took some. Then Mrs. Cartwright looked up and bravely addressed Ron's kids. *How's freshman year, Gwen?*

Oh, um. Gwen looked stunned to be addressed. *It's good. Thank you, Mrs. Cartwright.*

Please, she said. *Julie.*

Julie, Gwen said. Relieved by the sound of her own voice, Gwen began telling an interminable story about a class she had with her roommate, or at least a class they *thought* they had together, until her roommate realized she was supposed to be in another section of the class . . . *It was SO funny,* she said.

We'll take your word for that, Dean said.

Mrs. Cartwright turned to face Dean. *I'm glad you and Kirsten haven't really broken up, Dean. Have you set a date?*

Oh, no, not yet, Dean said. *I think it's going to be a little more of a conceptual engagement for a while.*

Mrs. Cartwright took a bite of her plain salad. She hadn't even brought out dressing. *That's probably good. No sense rushing these things.*

I Tami, said Tami to Claire.

I know you are, sweetheart, said Claire. *And I'm*—she fought back tears—*Claire.*

By then all four children had felt it.

A lightening. A warm release. Nothing less than the grace Charlie had asked for.

For several minutes no one spoke. But they were all thinking the same thing: the Widow Cartwright's generosity had returned this disastrous meal to a celebration of gratitude and family.

Of mercy.

And that's when the front door flew open and a massive sixty-year-old woman in a leather bomber jacket—Mrs. Cartwright's AA sponsor, Sybil, as it turned out—stalked into the room, eyes wildly casting about as if she'd lost her mind, screaming like a drill sergeant at the Madden children: *What ... the FUCK ... is the matter with you people?*

CHAPTER 7 | DESSERT

When it was over, the boys sat outside their father's new house, on the curb next to Dean's car, drinking Charlie's pie.

They'd broken off an edge of pie crust and slurped the sugary chocolate pecan whiskey mixture over the side of the pan. It was actually kind of delicious. It reminded Dean of a root beer float once the ice cream had melted—but with a little whiskey kick.

I think you could bottle this, Dean said.

I still can't believe it, Charlie said.

He was referring to the news Sybil had unloaded on the kids after a quick prologue about their selfishness and self-absorption and the very real danger they'd put poor Julie in—all punctuated with various versions of the word *fuck*. She called them *fuckwits* and *fuckchops* and *fucking heaps of fuckless dog shit*. Then she turned on Ron.

And you—limp, lifeless, worthless fuckfruit, you raise these shitty humans and then let them run wild on the woman you LOVE?

The Widow Cartwright put her hand up to get Sybil to stop, but there was no stopping Sybil. *Shut! The fuck up! Julie! If you and milquetoast won't tell these entitled little fuckquats, then I will. Hey kids! Guess what! Your mom's a lesbian. Know how I know? 'Cause I fucked her! Me and every other dyke in town! You know the last time your dad and mom had sex?* She pointed at Gwen. *Nine months before little Sunbeam here came into the world. But you know what your parents did? They took one for the team! For YOU! They played house and got what they needed on the side, and they waited until you'd lived your little Pleasantville childhoods, then they went to find the tiniest bit of happiness for themselves!*

Dean flashed on the name of the cruise ship their mother was on: the *Sapphic Rose*. Right, he thought.

Sybil swept her arm across the table, sending boozy brussels sprouts and shrimp salad flying. *I am so tired of this! We treated you like the center of the universe, tiny little princes and princesses, we drove you to soccer and cheerleader camp and hired you SAT tutors! The whole world was built for YOUR comfort, YOUR entertainment. Daddy wiped your privileged ass, Mommy pumped breast milk to make your fucking macaroni and cheese—*

That was when Dean and Charlie first made eye contact.

And it's when Sybil's rant started going sideways, aimed not just at the Madden kids but perhaps at an entire generation, yet also at some personal experiences she'd apparently had, maybe as a mother or an aunt. It was hard to catch it all: apparently she'd gone out with a younger girl who'd cheated on her. And she loaned her nephew her pickup, and he returned it with a big dent. By the time she got to the misogyny of the TV show *The Bachelor* even she must have realized she was off point. She spun on Gwen. *You have five seconds to apologize before I drag your pixie ass out of that chair and into the street.*

Gwen immediately turned to Julie. *Sorry!*

Sorry! they all said. *Sorry, sorry!*

I Tami, said Tami.

Claire wept.

Things settled down after that. Sybil helped clean up, and Julie walked her to the door, hugged her, thanked her.

She seems effective, Dean said.

There was nothing to do but finish dinner. Through it all, the Widow Cartwright—Julie—was never less than charming and warm. Ron couldn't seem to close his mouth. They had coffee and moved to the living room, where Tami dragged a picture book around for each Madden kid to read to her. It was about a lonesome boy who befriends a wolf. *Read me!* Tami would yell, shoving the book into their hands, as if she had, at that very moment, just invented a use for this collection of words on pages between boards.

All four kids left at the same time. Exhausted, Ron and Mrs. Cartwright—*sorry, Julie*—didn't press them to stay longer. Julie hugged each one at the door while Ron stood holding Tami. The Madden kids felt an unusual pride: that their father was the kind of man who would help raise this sweet little girl.

After Claire and Gwen drove away, Dean said he needed a drink. That's when Charlie remembered his pie. So they sat at the curb, slurping shots of chocolate pecan whiskey.

And if they didn't *exactly* talk about what they'd just gone through—the experience of having been redeemed through their shame—it wasn't because they didn't feel it. Perhaps people sometimes lack the common language to discuss such things. Instead, the boys debated how much breast milk a woman would have to pump to make a proper box of macaroni and cheese. Finally the pie pan was dry, and the brothers stood. They took one more look at their father's new house, at his new life. Warm yellow light glowed behind the heavy curtains.

I Dean, said Dean.

I Charlie, said his brother.

W. C. FIELDS TAKES A WALK

PAISLEY REKDAL

Alone, I march with my ruined mouth, plaid vest
stinking of whiskey. Alone, with my little vial of pain
rattling at my leg. People want me
to say something funny and I tell them, *Only privacy
amuses me. You want funny, break a bone
and sing through it.* That's my nameplate,
calling card: fat man, drunkard, turnip-
face: rage's endless, hectoring joke.
Fans pretend they can't believe it, insist
it's all a game: they call me Santa
in the gossip pages, they call me Naughty
Chickadee. But it's the lion they like,
roaring and bleeding, their timid fists
rapping at my cage. Fame
means accepting you can be only one story.
I like to stand backstage, jeering at the coal-
scrubbed comics who won't make it,
laughing at their quivering
cheeks, their still-white mouths, and shout,

You don't believe it! The vaudeville girls,
I thought they'd get it, with their champagne
curls, breasts leoparded with sequins. But too soon
they slip offstage to wipe the grease
paint off, unpin their dresses, kiss their kids,
and let their figures go. They're tired,
they say. After all those shows. Tired women, tired
like my mother with her German cheekbones,
papery and yellow. At the stores, she could barely
rouse herself to act Camille half the time,
the other half like Garbo. While at home
she never knew what to be, wringing her hands
by the kitchen stove, *Too sensitive*, she said,
to the sad slow beat of my heels
drumming on the carpet. She said
she wanted life to be something *realer*
for herself. Me, I can walk a mile with a nail in my boot
and a smile on my face. I can walk
until the metal drills into my sole.
I shake my vial with its jabbering pills.
I stroke my coat, bathe myself in perfumes of cigar smoke.
I pour whiskey into my whiskey.
Then I pour it down my throat. Once, joking
with the boys by Dempsey's locker, a group
of rotted teeth fell out. And Dempsey winced!
Tried to look away. (I'm proud to say
the space still gapes: I never got a bridge.
Why hide? That gap is me now, all the way.)
Champ, I warned the boxer, *that kind of girlishness
will get you in the end.* And then
I stuck my tongue through that bloody place
and sang "La Marseillaise."

THE LONELY MARTHA

Everybody knows George Washington cut down his father's cherry tree with a hatchet and couldn't lie about it. What most people don't know is that he also chopped off Thomas Jefferson's hands—with a gator knife—and then pretended he didn't. Jefferson was furious, of course. He took a glove between his teeth and threw it to the floor at Washington's feet. Everyone was really sad and surprised about Jefferson killing Washington with a dueling pistol when he didn't even have hands, but then Benjamin Franklin bucked America up by inventing electricity and a classic craft cocktail called the Lonely Martha, slightly modified for our modern times below.

MAKES 2 COCKTAILS

A shrub	Whiskey	1 orange
A hatchet	Sweet vermouth	2 cherries
Dueling pistols	Something to muddle	Bitters

1 Find a shrub and chop it down with the hatchet. Admit that you've chopped it down. Open the case of dueling pistols. Close it. Make a Manhattan. I usually use bourbon, but you can also use rye. People in Wisconsin use brandy. No one knows why. The proportions are like this: 4 to 1 whiskey to vermouth. Or 10 to 1. Depending on how strong you want it. Some people will insist a Manhattan must be served up. That ice must not melt in it. Open the case of dueling pistols. These people should be shot. But wait: you're making a cocktail. Muddle whatever it is you're going to muddle. Pour the whiskey and vermouth over ice

or into a shaker. Stir it. Shake it. Stir it. I don't actually ever shake it. I stir it with my finger. Make yours however you want. Once the ice starts reacting with the whiskey, peel the orange into the garbage can. Citrus doesn't belong in a Manhattan. Cherries do. Get the good kind—the kind that don't look toxic. Dash in some bitters. Sip your drink. Admire the pistols. This is America. Sip again. Is the current president doing anything right? Who knows. Sip your drink and imagine how idiotic your face would look on money.

CHOCOLATE PECAN PIE WHISKEY SHOTS

While caramelized pecan pie filling is still hot, it can be smooshed into a shot-glass shape and then cooled, painted with melted chocolate, and filled with whiskey. You'll need a standard muffin pan and muffin cups, a culinary brush or offset spatula, and a tart press or something similarly shaped. Shoot the whiskey; eat the glass. For those holidays we can't remember to regret.

MAKES 6 TO 8 SHOTS

8 ounces finely chopped pecans (a little less than 2 cups once prepared)
¼ cup honey
1 tablespoon water
¼ cup sugar

¼ cup cream
2 tablespoons golden syrup (Lyle's, or use Karo syrup in a pinch)
1 tablespoon unsalted butter
1 teaspoon salt

½ teaspoon vanilla extract
¼ teaspoon ground cloves
4 ounces dark chocolate, chopped roughly
4 to 6 ounces bourbon or rye

1   In a medium bowl, put the chopped nuts. Grease a standard muffin pan, and set both aside.

2   In a medium sauté pan over medium heat, bring the honey and water to a simmer. Continue to simmer, stirring occasionally, until brown and nutty, 1 to 2 minutes.

3   Add the sugar, cream, syrup, butter, salt, vanilla, and cloves. Increase the heat to medium high and bring the mixture to a boil. Cook, stirring occasionally, until the mixture is darkened and caramelized, 5 to 8 minutes. It should be molten, bubbly, and thick, but not burned. Remove the pan from the heat. Pour the caramel over the nuts, and stir until evenly coated.

4   Immediately fill each muffin cup with about ¼ cup of the mixture, place
     a muffin liner on top, then, using a tart press or the end of a wooden
     spoon, press the mixture to create cups. If there are any holes in the floor
     or walls of the cups, use a little more of the nut mixture to patch them.
     Discard the muffin liners. Chill for 10 minutes in the refrigerator, then
     remove the pecan cups from the muffin tin and place them on a large
     plate or baking sheet. Set aside.

5   In a small microwave-safe glass bowl, place the chocolate and microwave
     on medium for 2 minutes. Stir. Microwave again in 15-second bursts,
     stirring in between each, until the chocolate has melted. While the
     chocolate is hot, brush the insides of the pecan cups with it. Chill the
     cups in the refrigerator for another 10 minutes, then brush them with
     another layer of melted chocolate. Set the cups aside to cool in the
     refrigerator again, about 10 minutes.

6   Once the cups have cooled completely, fill them with whiskey. They'll hold
     between ½ and 1 ounce of liquor, depending on how high and even their
     walls are.

7   Drink immediately; eat at your leisure.

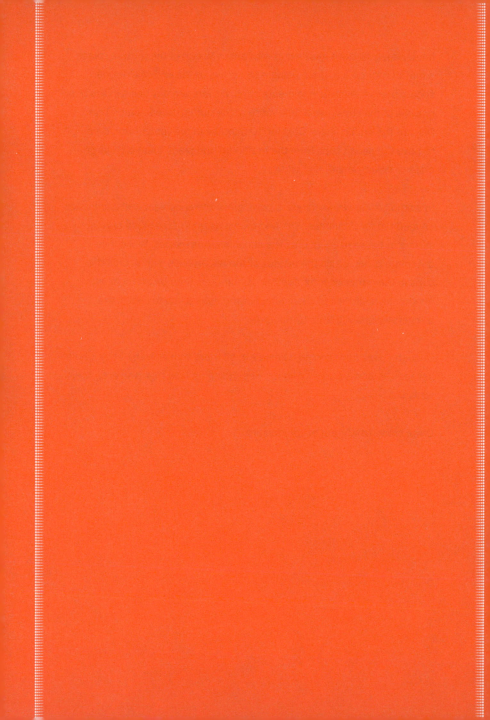

Always carry a flagon of whiskey in case of snakebite, and furthermore always carry a small snake.

—W. C. FIELDS

THE CAPTAIN'S DELIGHT

LAURA READ

When the DJ plays "Take It to the Limit,"
you think of your father. How he used to sing
along with the radio when this song came on,
his voice deep and unrolling. How he waited until
you were grown before he finally moved out,
bought a trailer, started taking dance.
When you visited him, he put a record on
and showed you what he was learning.
You were angry at him then
for leaving your mother,
but he died so soon after that now you're glad
he had the chance to stand between his Formica table
and his television, his arms open.
You sat on his thrift store couch, more threadbare
than the one you had in college, and watched him
turn an invisible woman, her ghost whitening,
dress tight, her hair thickly curled with an iron.

All his life he worked in a garage and came home
to a wife who left the TV on
when she went to lie down. It was the kind of house
where you couldn't bring friends,
all those small mirrors blinking in the living room,
how plates stayed on the counter long after dinner.
In the evenings, he lay under the cars
parked on your front lawn, slid out from under them
when you came out to ask for the keys.
He said the engine light's coming on in that one,
but you took it anyway. It rode wide and low
like this boat where you're dancing and drinking
a drink called the Captain's Delight,
orange and red like the sun going down,
three shots of whiskey slipped inside it. Strangers
keep handing you cigarettes, and you smoke them
off the side, flicking ash in the water.
Don Henley is singing every note slow,
and the lake is still, the moon's wet face full
and rising inside it, and you know
he would have loved to see you like this.
He would have asked you to dance.

LAURA READ

HEAVENLY PIES

ANTHONY DOERR

HER FATHER MADE PIES. Or he owned the corporation that did, anyway. Every convenience store carried them: Heavenly Peach, Heavenly Lemon, Heavenly Cherry Berry. Twice as Nice in Paradise. They came in four-ounce double-serving portions sealed in jade-green wrappers, and the *H* in *Heavenly* was drawn like a hurdle with a winged pie flying over the crossbar.

Mother didn't let me eat them. "No pie," she'd say, "should sit on a shelf for a year and stay golden brown. It's not natural."

We dated sophomore year: me and Janie Heavenly. She was six foot one and ultrarich, and people said she was slutty—even the nice kids said that—but Janie had big sad eyes and a way of looking off into the distance, as if at a grand passenger liner sailing off without her, that made me long for her.

Plus she had a big black Jeep with twin subwoofers. Most evenings, after school, I'd pedal my bike up the long, switchbacking road to Heavenly Hill, and her father would call me into the backyard and make me putt on his backyard putting green. I'd knock my ball into the pachysandra while he'd drain fourteen-footers and proclaim things like, "Men are like bank accounts, Jimmy. Without a lot of money, they don't generate a lot of interest."

Then Janie would tell Mr. Heavenly we were off to a movie, but instead we'd drive the logging roads east of town and park on some nameless ridge and put on *Genesis Live* and watch armies of clouds march across the valley. Her glovebox was always full of pies, and I'd eat four or five of them (golden crust and fruity goop), and Janie's mouth would taste like cinnamon and shortening, and after a while she'd stop kissing and push my head down and I'd do my thing between her thighs for as long as it took.

Afterward she'd sit with her jeans unzipped and look off into the horizon and say something like, "I cannot wait to leave this fucking place."

At school I'd slip cartoons into her locker.

A T. rex saying: *Rawr means I love you in dinosaur.*

A paratrooper saying: *Do you have a Band-Aid 'cause I just scraped my knee falling 4 you.*

She never sent cartoons back.

Everyone said it would end badly, and it did. I pedaled up Heavenly Hill one afternoon and Janie answered the door with lipstick all over her face. She said she had Fudgie Klapman in her bedroom and she was going all the way with him and probably more. "Probably a lot more," she said and shut the door. I'd never even seen Janie's bedroom. Her father waved his putter at me from the side gate in a friendly way, but I rode down the hill and skipped school for five days straight.

That was twenty-seven years ago. I ended up marrying Marsha McDonald. We have two daughters. I'm director of the branch library. Marsha doesn't like for me to eat her pie, or maybe I just never learned how to do it properly.

Every year the library budget shrinks, but this year it has been microscopic. We forgo heat, Kleenex, dental benefits. Still the board says we need to lay off three of the four librarians.

I make PowerPoint slides; I put on a gingham necktie and chum the private sector. A brewery donates twelve hundred. The semiconductor manufacturer donates two grand. It's not enough.

The board says, "You'll have to lay them off on Friday."

I say, "What about Heavenly?"

"Since the old man died," they say, "the Heavenly daughter hasn't given a cent to anyone."

"She's a taker, not a giver."

I say, "I have a connection."

From my desk I watch Barb Peterson help a homeless guy with the computer. I watch Slow-Motion Ken stock new magazines. Both of them have worked here since I was a kid.

I call the Heavenly Corporation and work my way up to Janie's assistant. She puts me on hold for a half hour. Then she says Janie would like to meet in person, at her house, how about Friday?

Things from adolescence are supposed to seem smaller when you revisit them, but on Friday afternoon Heavenly Hill seems twice as high. Only two of the twenty front windows are lit. Janie herself comes to the door. She's missing an earring, and her hands are as big as phone books. I give her the spiel, show her the PowerPoint. She stops paying attention halfway through.

"The trans fats thing is killing us," she says. "It's more legal now to smoke weed than it is to eat our pies."

Her eyes: wet, unreachable. What was it that I did for her, I wonder, on those summer nights? Did she ever feel, at the height of things, that we were chasing some glowing truth that stayed forever just out of reach?

She takes a bottle of whiskey from a shelf. "Stay awhile."

"I'm supposed to go fire people."

"Want to see my bedroom?"

The big house is utterly silent. I hear Phil Collins clear his throat. Big, round pies fall from the sky and explode in the driveway. I consider it: blowing up my life. Quit the library, marry Janie, putt on the putting green. Maybe draw cartoons again. Eat whatever. Twice as Nice in Paradise.

"I loved you," I say and make for the Subaru.

In the driveway Janie's hands fall to her sides. She looks eight feet tall. "I felt something, too," she says. "But I didn't know what it was."

I'm halfway to Slow-Motion Ken's when a text comes from the treasurer. The Heavenly Corporation, he says, is donating seventy thousand dollars. *That must be some connection*, he writes.

I take my family to Five Fathers Pizza and order a jug of cabernet. I toss croutons into my daughters' open mouths.

Marsha says, "What's got into you?"

I blow her a kiss over the pepperoni.

On the way home I stop at Ready-Go and pull four pies from the Heavenly rack. Little Katie chooses apple. Molly takes Cherry Berry. Marsha cocks her head, like she's trying to figure out if she should disapprove. I tune the radio to K-Rock, hoping for Genesis, and we sit, the four of us, in the glow of the gas station lights, Heavenly Hill invisible in the darkness beyond, and peel back the bright-green wrappers.

DRINKETH THOU NOT THE ALCOHOL DRINK

NICOLE SHEETS

MY CHILDHOOD WAS SET in the King James Bible. It was full of regal words like *diadem, countenance, soothsayers, seraphim, concupiscence.* It was full of rules like "Taketh thou not too many wives" or "Generously tippeth thou thy manservants and maidservants" or "Drinketh thou not the alcohol drink."

I was a child in a small church in West Virginia. We read the King James Bible and sang from hymnals with notes shaped like Lucky Charms. The church covenant forbids the alcohol drink. So what if the King James Bible warns about drunkenness, not the drink itself? The church plays it safe. Drinketh thou not the alcohol drink.

The "fruit of the vine" that Jesus drank was the same grape juice consumed during communion, on the first Sunday of the month. On the first Sunday of the month, this is how you obtain the grape juice: from an usher you take a round, heavy silver tray ringed with tiny plastic communion cups. With care, you lift your cup. You stare at the grape juice. You think about the blood of Jesus and the sins of sinners. You hold the cup between your fingers until the pastor reads, "For as often as ye eat this bread and drink this cup, ye do shew the Lord's death till He come." Then you shoot your grape juice and slide the cup into the appropriate hole.

On the backside of each pew, next to a rack for Bibles and hymnals, are two small holes side by side, fitted with rubberized rings. This sounds like some kind of vintage contraception, which the church does not forbid but also does not discuss.

After communion, children rove the holes and collect the cups in sticky towers for the ushers. I don't know what happens to the cups. I do know that grandmothers take Styrofoam balls the size of whopping cantaloupes and cover them with plastic communion cups. The grandmothers rim each cup in glitter.

Verily, behold, when I was a child, I drank like a child. I drank childish things like fruit punch and Sierra Mist. Now that I am a man, I drink like a man. I drink the alcohol drink.

As a man, I favor proverbs over commands. Proverbs give you wisdom like *Beer before liquor, never sicker.*

Stick with beer, you're in the clear.

Drink seven glasses of wine in Stacy's backyard, and the vomit on your chest will startle you awake.

I've learned to conjure all kinds of spirits, like gin, marshmallow vodka, rum with pirates on the bottle, tequila, whiskey.

I've learned to say thank you when Jeremy the basement guy leaves us a mason jar of Fireball whiskey. I unscrew the lid and take a slug of its cheap sweetness and heat. I like the burn.

When I drink whiskey, I feel as though I'm sinning and paying for my sin at the same time. It's an efficient way to sin.

Sloth is not my kind of sin. Drunkenness, your general riotous living, those are my kinds of sins.

The whiskey makeout in Jeff and Jenny's computer room while the rest of the party grinds their plastic Halloween costumes on the dance floor, that's my kind of sin.

When I drink the alcohol drink, I feel both dirty and clean.

I feel clean because alcohol is a known disinfectant. Maybe I don't need an old-time tooth extraction. Maybe I don't have a Civil War bullet lodged in my haunches, but I could use a little propping up.

Whiskey makes me feel dirty because ladies don't order whiskey. Ladies don't drink, but if they drink it's something lame like a wine cooler or fancy like a flute of champagne.

Whiskey means my friend Molly shouting, "How does a West Virginia girl hold her liquor?"

"I don't know," I say.

"By the ears."

Whiskey makes you say things like that.

Whiskey means business. Whiskey means a buzz just isn't good enough.

DANCE

SHERRIE FLICK

VIVIAN SIPS HER WHISKEY in the den where her thoughts waver between doom and joy. In her mind, Viv has always had a tumbler of whiskey in one hand. Her other hand waves in conversation like a tiny bird. That hand used to habitually hold a cigarette, but not anymore.

Vivian is slumped into the leather chair, worn in the right places. She's half in shadow, half in light. After she retired from her teaching job, all of that schoolbook knowledge settled inside her like a sand dune. Ideas and concepts flit through her thoughts, shimmer and dull. She picks up her book. Sets it down.

Vivian whispers, and her voice cracks as it carries down the hallway, asking Matty to get her more ice for her drink. He always hears her, eventually. By the time he shows up, cubes dripping through his clawed fingers, Viv is repeating, "Ice, ice, ice," letting the *sssss* slide through her front teeth like a piece of stretched ribbon.

Matty plunks the sweating cubes into the glass. Ploink, ploink, ploink. Ploink.

"Always with this drama, Viv. Really," he says. "You could walk down the hallway yourself and get the damn ice." Then, glancing at the wall beyond the windows, he says, "You know, y'all shouldn't be day drinking like losers in here. At least try the patio. Jesus." Matty brushes a few crumbs from his apron. Viv watches as they fall like little shooting stars to the floor between them. His apron is lime green with bright-white flowers, a ruffle along the neckline. It once belonged to Viv. Now that Matty has sold his construction company, the apron's ties wrap his thick middle with a bow.

"There's just one of me, Matty. Who in the hell you talking about with 'y'all'?" Vivian flits her hand, follows the expanse of the den wall— its sports trophies, hardbound books, and taxidermied deer head.

Matty nods at the deer. "I'm including Mr. Bojangles in my musings. Those eyes beg for some inclusion. At minimum." He pats the deer's nose, which looks convincingly wet and alive. The deer head is from a different time in his life. It has an air of archaeological remains and helps assure Matty that it wasn't always like this.

After he retreats to the kitchen, Viv lifts the deer head from its nail, leaving a ghost shadow on the rosy wallpaper. She carts it to the patio with her drink. She likes how it weighs down her free arm. She's surprised at its weight as she shuffles out into the clear light.

Mr. Bojangles looks both unhappy and unimpressed when she props him up in the metal chair. A dragonfly explores the air space above his ears, then flits away.

"I don't give one flying fuck," she tells the deer. Viv sits up straighter to accommodate this sentiment. The deer winks at her. But Viv won't give into that kind of flirtation. She reaches to pet its nose like Matty did but reconsiders. "Your eyelashes are fake," she tells the deer. "They are fake," she assures herself, blinking. She wants to pour the deer a drink. Instead, she has a good stare down with him. She's sure Mr. Bojangles is judging her. "Fucker," she says. She taps her fingers on the edge of the patio table, her nails making the tiniest drumroll on the stiff metal. "I know what you need," she says, and Viv shifts the deer so it's sitting in profile, waiting for its deer friends to arrive. "Better?" she asks, then settles into her own patio chair and her own thoughts, wandering from Proust to Previn to Picasso.

"It is decent-er on the patio, don't you agree?" she asks the deer after a time. The air is clear, and the waxy sound of crickets mixes with light traffic noises. The pretty potted plants Matty has tended to, overtended to, really, sit silently sober like overdressed introverts come to the wrong party. Vivian gives them a long look, wraps one leg over another, and squints at the view. A wooden fence and a brick wall are all she can see, and she can hear some neighborhood children, girls, squealing with delight in the distance, playing some kind of game. Tag? Bloody Murder? She can't tell.

Viv shakes her head, which clears it a little. She flips her unruly hair behind her shoulders. Her hair was once a vibrant, head-turning copper. Viv was a stunner. She knows this. "I used to turn heads, Mr. Bojangles," she whispers. She pats at her curls. "What brings you to this little outpost, anyway?" she asks, reaching her free hand across the table, tapping a finger to get the deer's attention.

Viv's pantsuit is terry cloth. The sunny yellow with its white piping gave her a blip of cheer this morning when she pulled it on over her skinny thighs. Her bony hands are loaded down with ruby rings, one on each finger. Her birthday, July. Ruby, her stone. Blood, blood red, she thinks. "Don't even," she says to the deer. She takes the rings off, setting them on the table like a wager. She wishes she had a deck of cards.

It's late August. Viv sucks at her whiskey. She sucks at an ice cube. She jiggles the glass. "It's watered down now," she confesses to the deer. She knows early evening is coming, because the state of her tumbler is a clock she reads like a sundial.

Inside, Matty looks out the window at Viv. She's leaning toward the deer like they're conspiring. The light from the nearby apple trees dapples the table and chairs like a school of fish. Matty knows he's been more productive since the incident. "Meeting goals," he tells the dough he's kneading. He rocks it firm and steady for tomorrow's bread. "It's been years now," he tells the kitchen. The dough transforms from sticky to elastic under his thrusting floured palms. Viv drinking and reading while he bakes and cooks is a good solution for them these days. He kneads the dough, rolls crusts, slices apples, peaches, and pears. He bakes and bakes, and the minutes pass like magic tricks he's seen a thousand times but never ceases to be amazed at. A fine puff of flour rises when he swats his belly.

Matty sips at the cooking sherry. No one is watching. He nestles the bread dough into a bowl for a slow rise. He plop-plops some of the sherry into the sliced pears a pack of neighborhood girls dropped off yesterday. He fingers in some nutmeg. He works the pears toward his pie. Translucent slices, the sweetest sugar dissolving, daring that crust to come closer. Most likely the girls stole the pears from a neighbor's tree while that person was at work. The girls can be sneaky and conniving, especially when they get roaming in a group like that. They steal berries from the alleyways, tomatoes from gardens, and sometimes a bottle of gin from a stash in someone's cellar.

The girls come and go up the front porch steps, dropping off what they're given to deliver: apples, concord grapes, fresh mint. Their mothers make them do it, and then they make the girls go back with dollars folded into the soft spaces of their tiny front pockets to buy the pastries Matty bakes. He takes orders every Monday. He's tacked up a chalkboard on the far wall to keep track of everything. He lists his regulars, lists his fruits and nuts, lists what he plans to bake. The girls run off to tell their moms, and the moms call their orders in to Matty. They talk quickly and quietly on the phone as if they don't want their husbands to hear, as if they're telling him a secret. Sometimes they ask him for something special, like these hand pies. Matty always says yes.

Every Friday, he wipes the board clean and starts over again.

Matty crimps the soft top crust to the bottom, pinching the dough into a zigzag around the pan. He has carved a few delicate flowers on the top crust as steam vents for the baking pie. The flowers are in the shape of daisies. It's a bundled nest of lush sweetness when he's finished sealing it up.

He brushes some milky water over the top, slides it into the oven. The oven's heat slaps at Matty's face, scorches his arms. He clicks on the timer, then gently stacks the sugary hand pies he finished earlier in the day into a paper sack. He eats one. Can't help himself. Raspberries, brown sugar, and walnuts with a tiny bit of mascarpone. He's gaining weight, he knows.

The breeze shimmies the treetops outside the kitchen window. They flip and flop in the late-day sun. A gorgeous day, and Matty finds himself dancing across the linoleum floor. He hums to the shaking trees' rhythm, twisting his bulging hips and sliding a slippered foot. He pumps his arms, smoothes the kitchen air with his hands. As he pivots near the dishwasher he remembers those dark nights at the bar with Viv, disco dancing until two. They owned the place. That blood-red hair of hers, always a beacon, bringing him to shore. They'd hug their hips to the bar afterward. Ordering another final, final round. Bonfires at the ocean on weekends, out beyond the dunes and the rutted lane. Bright, big smiles with heads thrown back. Teeth, laughing, shadows. And then in the fire's shadow he's not sitting with Viv anymore. She's not sitting with him. The whole world had a different sheen back then. It was all Technicolor and denim. Driving with Jane, with Dee-Dee, no regrets, windows down like in a movie. The sun blip-blipping their soundtrack. Salty air. Seagulls. That sour taste of Sarah's too-young skin luring him in. Keeping him for a time when it didn't seem wrong. Nothing did. And then that night on Fishbone Street. Fishtailing and the silence that comes before impact. The bright, soundless ring of before. But that's over now. Behind him. Behind them.

Outside the kitchen, the sound of screeching tires. No thud, just indistinguishable voices and some yelling. Just another close call.

It's a close neighborhood on St. Anthony Street. Viv and Matty have lived here a long time now. Matty's family goes way down around this block and up the next, although everyone is gone now but him. The neighbors still talk—not that much, and never to him about anything that matters. Never about the incident. Now, Matty feels just fine. That's the truth. He feels like he has been and always will be fine.

Lulu Smith, a neighbor's girl, trots up the steps, her hair a blond mane secured high on her head with a thick elastic. She catches him dancing alone, and Matty is embarrassed. He flattens his hand over his aproned belly, adjusts the collar on his shirt. He taps on the radio news as he says, "Well, howdy-do, Princess Blue?" The stern, practiced NPR voice makes everything around him dull down to a crisp gray.

Lulu adjusts her ponytail, looks quickly toward the screen door she has just come through. She radiates summer, swimming, healthy snacks. Her Adidas sparkle, her bright-white ankle socks just so. Her athletic shorts are snug, like she will never have a care in the world. Matty remembers that she might be on the tennis team. Or she likes horses. He can't remember which.

Lulu pops her gum. She does not pretend that she didn't see Matty dancing his way across the floor. "Hello, Mr. Matty," she says. "Mama says hello. She says to say hello to Mrs. Viv, too." Lulu pushes one foot slightly forward, probably a remnant position from ballet class. She has brought some rhubarb, big long sticks of it from her mother's garden, wedged into a plastic shopping bag. "Mom says to give you this." Lulu tilts her head, holds the bag like a bouquet of roses in her skinny arms.

Matty takes the rhubarb from Lulu, gets a whiff of its stringent, sour pie potential as he shifts the bag to the counter. He imagines the cup of sugar he'll pour over top once it's rinsed clean and chip-chopped into a bowl. He knows the rhubarb bits will suck the sugar in like greedy little bastards. He looks at Lulu, who is waiting for him to say something. Her porcelain skin catches the light, and Matty feels a longing, a now unfamiliar longing, that leaves him speechless for a moment. He's transported back in time and then instantly back to this moment here.

"Well," he finally says. "Here's those hand pies your mama special ordered." Matty brushes Lulu's fingers as he gives her the crisp bag of goodies. Their hands touch when he takes the moist bills from her. "If you see SallyAnn, tell her that her mama's pear pie will be ready tomorrow morning." Lulu takes note with a quick nod that sways her ponytail, and she's gone.

"Bye, Lulu," he says too quietly, because she has already trotted down the stairs back into her summer day.

Matty washes his hands. He wipes them carefully dry. He changes into a clean apron. He doesn't usually change into a new apron this soon and wonders why he's doing it now, but it feels nice—crisp and clean. This one sports a giant parrot down the front with a violent blue background. Who knows where it came from. He looks out to Viv again.

"And?" she yells from the patio.

"And what?" Matty yells back, pulling the long red sticks of rhubarb from the shopping bag that reads "Thank you. Have a nice day!" in bright-yellow cursive along its side. The rhubarb is crusted with a layer of fine sandy dirt. He wants to wash it clean right away. Wants to get going on it.

"How's the pastry chef?" Viv says.

"It was fine. I'm fine," Matty calls back, his voice cracking. "Lulu. Jenny's girl. She picked up those hand pies, dropped off rhubarb. She reminds me of a horse the way she trots around."

Viv grunts to acknowledge the observation. "Mr. Bojangles needs a drink," she shout-talks. "I'm drinking with a deer," she says.

Matty nods in Viv's general direction, happy Mr. Bojangles has been brought into play on the patio. He considers making the deer a drink. A nice dry martini. Gin. Or a gimlet. He cuts a piece of rhubarb from the stalk, runs it under bright, cold water, then sticks the stalk's end into the sugar bowl. He bites down and chews. The quick rush of sweet and sour in his mouth is exactly what he needs. He considers making himself a martini but decides he will drink a little more sherry. Maybe later on he'll have one, staring up at the full moon from the patio with Viv.

Matty measures flour, rubs in butter, preps scones for the morning. He zests a lemon, rubs its sharp sunshine into the sugar before adding it to the bowl.

Matty contemplates dinner. Sliced tomatoes with some blue cheese in a quiche crust. Fat, eggs, cheese, salt. The oven chugs along, almost always on these days when he's awake. He can't wait to smell that quiche baking. He'll add a side salad and make a fresh raspberry vinaigrette. As Viv shrinks to nothing he fattens himself up. He imagines flying up and out of this neighborhood like a big, fat hot-air balloon. He's already far away when Viv comes tottering down the hallway toward the kitchen. Her uneven slipper heels tip-tap on the wooden floor. She clears her throat, sets her tumbler down gently, carefully, in the sink.

Both hands free, she can't think of what to do or say next. She feels sad and vulnerable, naked in her own kitchen. Matty looks at her strangely, so she gives him a slow squeeze, a hug. She pulls Matty into her, feeling for his former body—the body she once knew—now buried under the pudge of Matty. She pushes into him, but he's not there. His middle gives way softly and then expands back. She steps away from the embrace, giving him a poke.

She remembers the day they bought Mr. Bojangles at the junk shop on Miller's Lane. The dust glittering in the dull light as they opened and closed the creaking front door. The shelves overstuffed. She felt like she was saving the deer head, bringing it into a better home, a more interesting life, as she pulled it down from a hook on the wall. She hugged his wide, furry neck in the front seat as they drove home past fields of fireflies.

She asks Matty if he remembers that day. The song "Mr. Bojangles" playing on the radio, and they named the deer like it was a pet. Then they hung him on the den wall, and their life went on in its crazy way until there was a little too much crazy, until the night he let Sarah drive. Sarah of the palest, finest porcelain skin. Sarah of the best drugs. Sarah laughing, driving the truck. Viv in the back seat making time with who knows who. It didn't matter who was who. She and Matty were unstoppable. Matty made the biggest mistake with Sarah, and their life as it had been going on came to a halt and pretty much stayed still. They have always survived while Sarah smashed through and out.

"You bet I do," says Matty, and it takes Viv a moment to realize what he's responding to. "How could I forget?" he says.

Now Viv hums the song softly to herself while Matty turns back to his world, the kitchen counter, cracking six eggs into a bowl, whisking them fast and fluffy with a clop-clop noise. Did they just hug? Doesn't matter. Matty has returned to his task at hand: quiche. His back straight, his shoulders stiff.

Viv pours herself a drink. "And one for my furry friend," she says. She returns to the patio, fresh drinks, bright clinking cubes. One in each hand. She shuffles down the hallway. She slinks; she slithers; she moves down the hall like a winter draft. She smells salt air, bears witness to the deepening shadows that announce evening. A whiff of pear pie follows close behind.

MY HOUSE IS YOUR AMERICAN GOTHIC HOUSE

KATE LEBO

THE AMERICAN GOTHIC HOUSE looks bigger on the inside than on the outside, as if years of playing background to famous paintings and tourist photo shoots shrank its white balloon frame but left the un-pictured interior as is. The house itself, built in 1882 for a family of ten, has never been a museum, but there's a visitor center across the street where tourists can dress up like Grant Wood's farming couple: apron and wig for the woman, overalls and pitchfork for the man. You can photograph yourself in *American Gothic* drag with the house behind you in correct proportion to the painting. You can buy a painting of the house by a local artist, or a postcard of Wood's original, or a postcard of Miss Piggy and Kermit parodying Wood's original. Then you can cross the plaza, walk the narrow farmhouse porch, and knock on the windows of the house you've come to see. You might find the tenant home, but unless it's a day the Pitchfork Pie Stand is open, you won't be welcomed inside. You will, however, find the tenant friendly. That's a rule, written into the lease Beth Howard signed with the State Historical Society of Iowa in 2010 when she took over tenancy of the place for 250 bucks a month. She *must* be friendly.

For four years Beth baked pie in the apartment-size kitchen and sold it on summer weekends to tourists. Her crust method was intuitive and casual. She knew the dough needed a three-to-one ratio of flour to fat, so she measured about two and a half cups and figured the other half cup would be absorbed when she rolled out the dough. She skipped the supposedly all-important step of letting the dough rest for an hour in the fridge ("It's a hoax perpetrated by the fussy on the fussy," she said), cut the apples directly into the pie shell, and sprinkled them with flour, sugar, and cinnamon, using her hands and eyes as measuring cups. The week I baked with her in Eldon, I saw her raise her strong, tanned, ringless hands repeatedly, palms forward, since visitors always want to know. "These are your best tools," she'd say. "No electricity required."

When I arrived for ten days in August 2011 to help make five hundred servings of pie in hundred-degree weather, the Kohler Company had just gifted Beth with a brand-new farmhouse sink in exchange for a video about her uber-American living and business arrangement. "Now that I've opened a pie stand in the American Gothic House," she says in the video, "there is no possibility of not having pie here. It's like I've created a monster." Before the Kohler cameras arrived, when Beth showed me her remodeled sink, she pulled on the faucet's detachable nozzle and said, "I can't be the only one who's noticed this looks like a horse cock."

Beth grew up in Ottumwa, sixteen miles away. In a past life she sold coffee beans in Kenya and was a PR executive for Microsoft. She wrote for *Self* and *USA Today* and *Shape*. She was married. Her husband's aorta ruptured while their divorce was pending, layering monumental guilt on top of monumental grief. During her many lives, she told me, she wanted to write a book. Near the end of *Making Piece: A Memoir of Love, Loss and Pie*, she describes finding the American Gothic House as a fork in the road she "hungrily chose" shortly after the first anniversary of her husband's death. "I could picture it already," she writes. "This place could be my writer's retreat—and this is where my writing desk will go." By the time I visited in 2011, Beth was an expert on Grant Wood's story, the house's story, the story of pie—three strands of art, history, and Americana she braided into a mediagenic tale of doing what Oprah says we *can* and what Rilke says we *must*: change our lives.

When it wasn't sweltering hot, Beth slept on the private side of the lace curtain in the Gothic window whose arches appear on church marquees, lamppost flags, and roadside attraction signs. No one knows why Charles and Catherine Dibble, the original owners, chose to adorn their otherwise perfunctory house with a window fit for a church. Its incongruity is the reason Grant Wood stopped to sketch the house in the first place.

Ever since *American Gothic* began its public life at the Art Institute of Chicago in 1930, no one can agree on whether Wood, a native son of Cedar Rapids who said he "had to go to France to appreciate Iowa," was glorifying rural Americans or making fun of them. If rural folks thought *American Gothic* was a paean to their way of life, aesthetes called the painting middlebrow. If urban aesthetes saw a gleam of irony in the old farmer's eye, heartlanders didn't appreciate the joke one bit. *American Gothic*'s durability in the face of all these interpretations—its capacity to inspire *and* fit them—has, over time, made it the most famous painting in America.

Unlike pie—which anyone can make—and unlike answers to what *American Gothic* is "really about," there's only one American Gothic House. Only one white clapboard mother of parodies and rip-offs and references. Only one real, physical place that embodies the ambivalence of Grant Wood's classic. Until I slept on Beth's red sectional in the front parlor, I had no reason to think the house was anything but a static image, something to be honored or mocked but not worked and lived in. I, like Beth, was a writer hungry for something to write about and a place to write it in. I came here because I thought, as a pie baker—as an American who deals in Americana—I might discover some kind of deep knowledge from participating in the making of one symbol within another. What I found was Beth.

By moving into the Gothic House and setting up her pie stand, she staked a private claim within an image that, like pie, has been reproduced and remade so many times, it's become public property. I used pie as a ticket to see inside that image and make something there, as Beth was doing by using her tenancy as the setting that framed her plot, character, language, and loss with the larger myth any piece of writing needs to make it through an editor's slush pile. Maybe that myth is middlebrow, and maybe Beth's use of it is self-serving. But so what? Artists in search of a subject seize what compels them.

American Gothic is a mirror prism. My version is an image that reduces us all to tourists, but in a way that brings the actual house to life. Beth's version is the plot twist she'd been looking for: by stepping into the painting and waving to us from the windows, she found a shape for her new life and a public to share it with.

Like the painting's interpretations, the house's ownership is multiple. It is the State Historical Society of Iowa's house in that they own the title. It was Beth's house while she held the lease and had all her furniture inside. It has been, since some indeterminate point before but definitely during and since Beth's life there, everyone's house—including mine. Tourists felt entitled to knock on windows, and they were entitled. Beth resented the invasion of privacy, as she should've. We all expressed our possessive feelings by playing dress up and taking photos. In 2014 Beth moved to California (as of this writing she's back in Iowa on a thousand-acre ranch), but while she lived her next memoir, she provided us with another way to see beyond the icon: a slice of pie under the tree out front. If the Pitchfork Pie Stand were open today, I'd recommend the Shaker Lemon.

JOHN BROWN'S BODY

At the Kansas State Capitol in Topeka, John Steuart Curry's mural *Tragic Prelude* depicts John Brown as a terrifying, glorious giant, twice the size of the people surrounding him, his arms spread wide, a Bible in one bloody hand, a rifle in the other, a pistol on one giant hip, a sword on the other. He's furious! He's enraged! Union and Confederate flags fly behind him over pioneers walking wagons west. Fires burn, tornadoes swirl, slaves cower, and Brown's hair stands straight up, as if he's just been electrocuted by the Union and Confederate dead he's stepping on. Everything is burning and coming apart under the gleam of his maniacal eye. When you think of the horror and the glory of it all, think of this painting and think of the song "John Brown's Body," which later morphed into "The Battle Hymn of the Republic." It begins likes this:

John Brown's body lies a mouldering in the grave

John Brown's body lies a mouldering in the grave

John Brown's body lies a mouldering in the grave

His soul goes marching on!

Glory, glory Hallelujah (× 3)

His soul goes marching on!

MAKES 2 COCKTAILS

A recording of "John Brown's Body"

A reproduction of John Steuart Curry's mural *Tragic Prelude*

Your soul

Something to moulder

Whiskey

Sweet vermouth

One rifle

One pistol

One sword

Bitters

2 cherries

A Bible

1   Put on the music, loud. Sing with it. Loud. Place *Tragic Prelude* in a place you can't ignore. Find your soul. Study it. March with it. Muddle whatever it is you're mouldering. Make a Manhattan. I use bourbon, but you can also use rye. In Wisconsin they use brandy. No one knows why. The proportions are 4 to 1 whiskey to vermouth. Or 10 to 1. Depending on how strong you want it. Some people will insist a Manhattan must be served up. That ice must not melt in it. Pick up the rifle, the pistol, the sword. These people should be executed. But wait: you're making a cocktail. Make the cocktail. Touch the Bible. Keep singing. March your worn-out soul around the kitchen. Weep for America.

RASPBERRY WALNUT MASCARPONE HAND PIES

You can make Sherrie's hand pies two ways. If you make them round, the pies won't explode in the oven as easily (something about round shapes an engineer could explain), but the mascarpone will blend in almost completely with the raspberries. If you make them like a turnover, in triangle shapes, they'll probably explode some, but the mascarpone will remain in a creamy layer. Both hand-pie styles layer tart raspberries with creamy mascarpone and chunky nuts, and are absolutely delicious.

MAKES 6 HAND PIES IF YOU MAKE ROUNDS, 4 HAND PIES IF YOU MAKE TURNOVERS

½ recipe Pie School Pastry Crust (see page 241)

6 ounces fresh or frozen raspberries

⅓ cup light or dark brown sugar

1 tablespoon all-purpose flour

2 teaspoons unsalted cold butter, cut into small chunks

Pinch kosher salt

Pinch ground nutmeg

4 to 8 tablespoons mascarpone

¼ cup walnuts, chopped small

Egg-white wash (1 egg white beaten with 1 teaspoon water)

Granulated sugar, for sprinkling

1   Prepare the dough. Let it chill in the refrigerator for at least 1 hour or up to 3 days.

2   Preheat the oven to 425 degrees F. Line a rimmed baking sheet with parchment paper (you'll thank me for this later when you don't have to scrub your pan).

3   In a medium bowl, mix the raspberries, brown sugar, flour, butter, salt, and nutmeg, and set aside. Do not stir the raspberries into a soupy mess. Just stir gently to combine.

4   Roll the dough as you would for a regular bottom crust, stopping once it is about ⅛ inch thick and roughly round.

5   **TO MAKE ROUND HAND PIES,** use a round 3¾-inch biscuit cutter to make rounds (twelve in all) for the tops and bottoms of six hand pies. While you prepare the bottom crusts, chill the top crusts in the fridge. Smear 1 tablespoon mascarpone over the center of each bottom crust, leaving plenty of dough bare at the edges. Sprinkle 1 tablespoon walnuts over each smear of mascarpone, then top with 1 heaping tablespoon raspberry mixture. Retrieve the top crusts from the fridge.

6   Place one top crust on each filled bottom crust and fold up around the circumference of the hand pie (about a ½-inch fold), then press the tines of a fork around the edge to seal.

7   **TO MAKE TURNOVERS,** cut the dough into quarters so you're left with four triangle shapes of roughly equal size. Starting 1 inch in from the inside (by which I mean the cut) corners of the triangles, smear 2 tablespoons mascarpone up the middle of the dough, stopping 2 or 3 inches before the other (rougher and wider) edge of the dough. Sprinkle 1 tablespoon chopped walnuts over each smear of mascarpone, then top with ¼ cup of the raspberry mixture. Fold the dough triangles in half over the filling so the hand pies resemble turnovers. Bring the edges of the dough even, trim the ragged outer edge so it's even and only 1 to 1½ inch of dough frames the filling on all sides (except that mascarpone-filled side, which is on a fold, not an edge).

CONTINUED

8   Fold the matched-up edges of the dough over themselves to create about a ½-inch seam. Seal by pressing all around the seams with the tines of a fork.

9   **NOW, NO MATTER WHAT SHAPE YOU CHOSE,** cut small vents in the top of each hand pie. You won't be able to finish each hand pie at the same time, so as you finish one, then another, freeze them until all the hand pies are ready to bake. Then brush their tops with the egg-white wash, and liberally sprinkle them with granulated sugar.

10 Line up the hand pies on the prepared baking sheet, and place them in the middle of the oven. Bake for 10 minutes, then lower the temperature to 375 degrees F and bake for 15 more minutes. The hand pies are done when their crusts are golden brown and their juices bubble thickly at their vents.

11 Cool the hand pies on a wire rack. Any leakage that occurred while the hand pies were baking will be left on the pan as you pick the cooled pies up. Eat warm or at room temperature. Store leftovers wrapped in a towel on the counter.

3

*Whiskey is all right in its place—
but its place is in hell.*

—BILLY SUNDAY

HAPPY HOUR

TOD MARSHALL

I'm weary of my usual Bud Light or Genuine Draft.
Give me an Amputation-with-a-Yellow-Umbrella-
beneath-the-Green-Moon, six shots of Did-Ya-
See-That-Sunset, a schooner of "Ooh, ooh, let's splash
in the stunning foamy mess of a waterfall." Give me
four of your half-priced appetizers—two each
of New-Found-Joy (w/ no sugar) and Bliss-of-the-Past
(w/ fry sauce). I'll also have some cheesy Nostalgia
Rings for later. And please pour me two drafts
of Skip-in-My-Step and a shot of What-Matters-Most
with a twist of No-Wisdom, No-Regret, No-Gotta-Be,
and to finish, something smooth yet harsh, a whiskey
to sip slowly with eyes closed, warm as the womb.
But please be quick, the sign says this ends. And soon.

MILES CITY

MARGOT KAHN

AT A CERTAIN TIME, the boots coming into the Bison Bar were crusted with shit. It was mid-April, late afternoon, and Louise and I had been there since god knows when. She'd picked me up at the library where I was killing time. She could tell I didn't belong there; I was just passing through. My boots were the giveaway: clean, crepe-soled Boulets with pink uppers half hidden beneath my jeans.

In the next room, a woman was half bent under a green banker's light, shooting pool by herself. "That's Franny," Louise said. "She's always here." Franny had lines in her face like the rings of a tree. She didn't look at anyone, kept her eyes on the prize, even as the door opened and the light fell in on us. The men at the door were cast in shadows until they got close enough that we could smell them. Wet wool, blood, tobacco, mud.

Merle took the stool to the left of me. Louise was on my right.

"Howdy, Merle," Louise said.

"Louise," he said, touching the brim of his hat and then extending a hand, bent up every which way, in my direction.

"Ma'am," he said. "Pleased to meet you."

He lifted his right foot onto the bar of the stool and some shit mud flaked off onto the floor.

The warm weather had been good for the calving, and most everything had been going as well as could be expected, a few gone sideways, a few so big they lost the heifers, the orphan calves grafted onto other mothers. Merle and Louise talked about this all across me, as if I were a fence post or an open window. Across me, over me, through me. I looked at Merle's hands and imagined them up inside me, up to the elbows, up to the shoulder, pulling me inside out. All those heifers, so heavy with purpose, and Merle, their deliverance.

I was making my way west again, the one place that pulled me. I'd left Ohio years before, gone west and then east and now back again. Ohio wasn't a place where I had deep roots, wasn't where my people long ago staked a claim. It was where my grandparents happened to land during the war, a place they dug in deep enough to give their offspring a chance, and for me that chance looked like someplace else.

Again the door opened, and the light was hanging on. This time, laughter. The seats at both ends of the bar filled, and the stool next to Merle was taken by a younger man in the same thick shirt, the same shit boots, the same hands, only slightly more limber. Merle's voice dropped, and now the conversation required fewer words. Full pints appeared before me and Louise. We looked to the right and then to the left, and they touched their hats to their brims and we smiled and lifted the new glasses to our lips.

The boys to the right were telling stories. The one about the kid who roped a bear down in Yellowstone, and the sheriff who came out and arrested him and took him in to jail. The kid went before the judge, and the judge said, "What were you thinking, roping a bear?"

The kid said, "Well, it's something I've always wanted to do, sir. And there he was, and I had my rope."

The judge said, "Was it hard?"

The kid said, "No sir. The roping wasn't hard. It was the lettin' him go that was difficult."

Louise invited me to stay the night at her place, a trailer on the edge of town, but the next time the door opened, the light had gone flat and the outside world was no longer a place we wished to be.

The cowboys who came in now had clean hats and clean shirts and belt buckles as big as pie plates. The tall one with the busted nose ordered a whiskey and tipped his chin in our direction.

"Louise," he said.

Even though she was an unashamed Democrat, a single woman in her thirties who lived alone, Louise had grown up here and was a part of this place in a way I would never be.

"Jude," she said. "Want to tell us about it?"

"Well," he said, turning so we could see the whole mess of his face. "It seems like every time I leave Montana, someone wants to kick my ass."

Louise laughed, but in Jude's voice I was here and there and going many ways at once. The break in his nose, the glint of his buckle, the cant of his boot heel resting so casually at the end of a long leg. There was the place I had left that would always be with me and the place, yet unknown, where I was going. If *home* was the place I had left behind, what would I call my place of becoming? Franny and Merle, Louise and Jude and me, we were, separately, these specks of light, small and shining. Franny was taking a cut shot; Merle and the others were filtering out into the evening, getting back to the heifers who couldn't be left alone. There were things in this world that were urgent and necessary, and all I could think was *Don't leave.*

THE LAW OF ATTRACTION

KIM ADDONIZIO

BECAUSE THERE MAY COME a time when you would like—no, really fucking want—to pour an adult beverage over your bare breasts in front of the person you are not with but would like—no, really fucking want—to be with.

Because you have imagined all the ways you could be with this person, but those are ways you have been with other people, and this person feels special so it has to be something new, something you have never done with anyone.

It gets harder and harder to find new things.

Those other people are always strangers. It's always late, after some bar has closed down, after you've closed down and turned off most of the lights in your head.

With other people it's kissing, both of you with your eyes shut—you open yours occasionally, quickly, which is how you know about theirs.

Then faking an orgasm to get it over with if they go on too long.

Then leaving as soon as possible.

Mostly, also, hoping you never run into one of those other people at, say, a dinner with mutual friends that you didn't know he was invited to. Watching him wait until you sit down, to make sure the two of you are at opposite ends of the table. It's drinking three margaritas, trying not to remember lying on your stomach naked, and him on his hands and knees behind you, complimenting your ass, and you reaching behind to get him off a second time because you're too drunk and tired to leave and you don't want him inside you again.

Then asking for a towel.

The person you want to be with would be different. He's not a stranger; you've known him, sort of, for several months now. He asks about you: *Did you get enough to eat today? Did you talk to your landlord yet about your broken oven?* He laughs when you say things. He says you're funny. *Funny ha-ha or funny peculiar? Funny ha-ha,* he says, and laughs again.

Other people don't say that. You make what you think is a clever remark, and they look at you like, That is weird. Like, How inappropriate. What is wrong with you?

The person you want to be with is married. If you could get him away from his wife, there would be a chance for you, but there she is, at work every single day. Wife taking a bagel delivery, wife ringing up a Harvest Chicken Salad, wife wiping off a table. He owns the restaurant. It's more like a deli, really, except there's a full bar. Shiny red booths, a dizzying floor of small black-and-red tiles. In the mornings, people come in for the bagels. There are eleven kinds. You can have any of them you want, for free. You can have cheesecake for lunch and take home a pastrami on marbled rye for dinner. You can have a drink or two if a certain bartender is working.

What you can't have is him.

He has touched you twice. Once he put his hand briefly on your hip when he brushed past you to get into the walk-in refrigerator. It felt like a hot iron on silk, like it would scorch you if he left it there a second longer. The other time he said, when you were removing a wedge from a peach pie, *Watch the hair*, and brushed it out of your face. You tie it back, but there is always a little that escapes. *Nobody wants a hair pie*, he said and laughed. *Sorry, that was totally inappropriate*, he said.

You looked up *hair pie* when you got home that night. It meant what you thought it might mean.

You need to choose an adult beverage. You have this fantasy about pouring a drink over yourself, but you're not quite clear on what the drink should be. You need to visualize; that's how you're supposed to get what you want.

Even though you never do.

What you want is to go into the walk-in with him and shake with cold all over except where he touches you.

Wine seems like a bad idea, because you wouldn't know which one to pick. Beer, also—too ordinary. Possibly champagne is a good idea. But there was that person who shook a bottle in your kitchen before popping it open so the champagne spurted up and poured down his arm. Which seems a little too close to what you have in mind, so not special enough.

And besides, you would like—no, really fucking want—to forget that person. That person who filled you up, before all the strangers. Who would have fixed the oven and then baked something in it. Rhubarb pie. Prosciutto chicken with mushroom sauce. Breakfast frittata.

Plain, poppy, sesame, onion, garlic, egg, salt, pumpernickel, whole wheat, asiago, cinnamon raisin.

The Law of Attraction, according to something called New Thought philosophy, is "like attracts like." In order to activate the Law of Attraction, you have to visualize.

There are three steps to the visualization. Step one is to pretend you are watching yourself in a movie.

You see yourself in the one where a man has come to Las Vegas to drink himself to death and meets a whore with a heart of gold.

In one scene they are on a lounge chair by a motel pool. She pulls down the top of her bathing suit and pours whiskey into her open mouth, letting it run over her breasts. He licks it off in slow motion in the gold sun.

Step two is to open a door in the screen and walk into the movie. You go in. There's whiskey left in the bottle, and that's what you'll use.

But now they've broken a glass table, and the manager of the motel is throwing them out.

Step three is to grab the screen and reduce it to the size of a cracker and swallow it. You try to imagine this, but it's confusing. If you're already in the movie, how can you grab the screen? And now, if you eat the scene, you are swallowing broken glass.

Also, feeling small and ashamed.

It's difficult to trust any advice that involves turning a movie screen into a cracker.

But still, whiskey.

You visualize the restaurant where you work. You see the person you want to be with kissing you, his hands on your face. You see that you could make this happen. You could call him into the walk-in for some reason, in the slow hours between lunch and dinner, when his wife sometimes leaves to run errands. Drink enough beforehand so that the lights in your head are turned low, little candle flames that don't throw any shadows.

Take off your shirt and bra and panties, but leave your skirt on.

Show him the bottle. Lift your skirt.

He is kissing your mouth, then licking the whiskey off your breasts like a magic potion that will bind the two of you forever. He tells you to turn around and bends you over beside the wire shelves that hold see-through plastic containers of oranges. You put your palms against the wall. He is fucking you and moaning. This is special and you are special. You are his whore angel. He's not a broken-down alcoholic trying to drink himself to death. He hardly drinks at all.

KIM ADDONIZIO

He loves his work. He loves holding your breasts, sticky with sweat and alcohol, and how you are making him feel.

But then you see what will happen afterward.

The hand towel grabbed from a hook, him refusing to look you in the eye.

You walking back out to serve pie and blintzes and sandwiches and sneak more whiskey. As much as possible. Your head too bright, headlights and zapping stars.

Him going past the tables, down the narrow hall to the men's room to wash his hands.

Wife leaning over the podium, crossing off names on the reservation sheet. Wife glancing at you as she picks up menus and leads a group to a four-top. Wife later that night, next to him in bed, him rolling her over.

You're not in the movie now. You're miles away.

You reduce the screen to the size of a pill.

Months ago you stole some OxyContin from a stranger's bathroom, after that person who used to fill you up disappeared, leaving a note on the refrigerator.

Sorry I can't anymore.

Because you used to feel new, like a freshly washed T-shirt, but now you feel like a rag that's been used to wipe off bread crumbs and ketchup spills and smears of cream cheese.

You swallow the pills.

Because it's the same shit over and over.

You take the giant bottle of whiskey out of the cupboard and sit in your favorite pajamas on a beach towel on your kitchen floor.

You open a door in the bottle. You go in.

THE MISSING <u>AND</u> FUCKING YEARS

STEVE ALMOND

I WAS TRYING TO get my wife to fuck me in the kitchen was the situation. Maybe I shouldn't say *fuck*. Maybe I should say *make love*. Language is such a racket. It's always pretending we can want only one thing at a time. But I wanted to make love to my wife while *also* fucking her kind of hard—in our kitchen. I wanted the tender panic of the thing, the writhing embrace. Maybe there's a German word. It was a Friday night. We were both completely thrashed. Our children had done this to us. We had four of them, a ridiculous number. But they were in bed now, sprawled out like little shooting victims.

Reagan was leaning against the counter, her ass outlined by a pair of pilled pajama bottoms. She did not in any way want to be fucked. No, she had it in mind to bake something for the cakewalk at the annual school picnic, an event that would obliterate any reasonable chance at happiness for our Saturday.

She didn't have to do this. There were going to be five hundred cakes for that goddamn cakewalk. She could have made one from a mix or bought one from our local Temple of Holy Organics. But that wasn't how she rolled. There were the other 499 moms to be considered, each of them bitterly devoted to an unspoken decathlon involving domestic duties they all claimed to loathe.

As for me, I was at the sink, working the scratchy side of a rotting sponge, because our dishwasher was on the fritz again. I kept staring over at Ray, imagining my stupid cock pressed into the canal formed by her ass cheeks. The house was quiet, except for my rhythmic scrubbing.

Then Ray canted her hips, and I set down my sponge and dried my hands and quietly approached from behind. "You're looking especially scrumdiddlyumptious this evening." I circled my arms around her waist.

She released a puff of pleased disdain. I wasn't supposed to touch her belly, which had itself grown a little spongy.

"Stop it," she said.

"Stop what?"

"Palpating my flab. Pressing your wiener against my butt."

Wiener I didn't like, as language goes, but *butt* worked just fine.

"Come on," I said. "Let's bring these two crazies together. Wiener and Butt. They should be friends. They should have a playdate."

"Seriously?"

She thought I meant anal sex, which I probably did. In my own head, over the past decade, I had written the libretto for an adult-themed opera entitled *The Anal of Figaro*, which involved Italian hair-care professionals in the throes of sodomy. Like every other man on earth, my urges had been disfigured by internet clips of women who greeted the penetration of their bleached and puckered rectums as a rapturous event.

Ray and I had tried a few times, early in the marriage, before procreation and grievance kiboshed our erotic adventurism. It had been a disaster, of course, but sort of sweet, too, very patient and lubricated. There had been one attempt in particular, the last, in which I had slowly nestled the tip of myself inside her, a brief chimerical era that ended after an ill-advised and hopeful thrust—not even a complete thrust, mind you, more of an exploratory nudge.

But I wasn't after anything like that. Honest. I just wanted to tug down those gauzy pj's and slobber on her privates for long enough that she might let me hump her, in whatever configuration she desired, in our poorly lit and pancake-batter-flecked kitchen.

This was something that used to happen quite a lot, by which I mean that it had happened exactly once before, fifteen years ago, in the mildewed rental Ray kept in Columbus, Ohio, where she had gone to get her degree in nutrition science. We had been dating long distance for a couple of years by then, the Missing and Fucking Years, as I thought of them, not unkindly.

"I get it," Ray said, swaying away from Eager Wiener. "You're horny."

"Horny for *you*," I purred.

"Please don't purr," Ray said.

"You're carrying a lot of stress," I said. "I can see it in your delts."

"You don't even know what delts are."

I started to rub the plump little knobs on either side of her neck, which were possibly delts. This she liked. "We should drink a little," I said. "And let nature take its course."

"*Nature* being the code word for your cock."

"*Nature* being code for the desires that bind man to woman."

"And man to man. And woman to woman."

"Hell, yes," I said. "Just keep the kids out of it."

"I've got to make this cake, Jake."

That was me. Jake the horndog. Jake the schmuck.

"So make the cake, and let me work my magic back here. I'll get the lavender oil and make everything slippery."

"You're sweet," she said, like I was a bag boy who'd helped her out with the groceries and was now awaiting a tip. In this analogy, the tip was having sex with me in the kitchen, and her response ("You're sweet") was her opting not to tip.

"I'm serious," I said. "Let's make a little nonsanctioned hanky-pank. I'll set up the compost thingy. I'll be your best friend."

"My best friend wouldn't sexually harass me."

"Remember how we used to do it in the kitchen?"

"I don't need another infected toe."

I had no idea what she was talking about. This was becoming a problem in our marriage. We had no idea what the other one was talking about much of the time. Our private servers of resentment and complaint kept hacking into public discourse.

I nuzzled the nape of her neck and slipped my hands beneath her pajama bottoms and began scratching her bum. Ray was itchy all the time: her scalp, her back, her butt, her ribs, her ankles. It was one of the plagues of motherhood, along with reflux and guilt.

I stood, abrading her pearly loaves with my nibbled nails. I didn't care what she looked like, the sags and pouches she'd acquired expelling four itsy humanoids out of her body. Evolution had equipped me with astonishingly supple standards. Not even a steady diet of porn, with its cantalouped anorexics and lithe cock gymnasts, had put a dent in my spousal desire. What I wanted wasn't an immaculate performance but the ancient crackle of lust, the half-blind and unsightly heaving.

Am I saying Ray was ugly? No, sir. She was lovely and plump and middle-aged. She had light-brown eyes and a slight underbite I affectionately referred to as her *womandible*. I myself had grown wretched: balding, pot-bellied, with a wattle of skin beneath my chin that our two youngest, the twins, who were three, yanked on with a devout and reliable hilarity. Nobody would have paid to watch us, but nobody had to. That was the whole point.

My scratching sent Ray's bouquet wafting up. She was a person of aromatic density. Tropical fruits and medieval herbs, the contrails of cleverly marketed ointments and shampoos, which mingled with top notes of sweat and womanly tang. I wanted to drop to my knees and spread her cheeks and slurp at whatever was within range of my slurper. But Ray didn't like when I did this. Even on our designated date nights I was discouraged from licking her below the waist. I was running out of erogenous options, frankly.

Ray had been raised in an angry Catholic suburb outside Pittsburgh, the only girl in a prefab full of cruel boys. Her brothers had teased her for being horny and smelly and gross, and these indignities had embedded in the soil of her mother's dogma. The devil was always trying to tempt children into defiling their bodies. That was why you needed to go to confession, so you could duck into a tiny darkened room and talk dirty to masturbating priests. Then you were forgiven.

Ray's father had been a Reagan Democrat, and her mother was crazy for Irish culture. That explained the name, which meant something like *the chosen lass* in Gaelic. They were from steel country, my in-laws, a couple of sweet fatsoes. I actually liked them quite a bit. They were terrific grandparents if you didn't expect too much. They brought meals to aged and crippled neighbors. They were virulent racists, too, but what the hell. Who isn't? Visiting them involved a lot of crucifixes. In every room, a naked little rabbi was nailed to the wall, perishing in gruesome hunkitude.

All this religious hokum had done things to my Ray. As a teen she'd skulked around in crop tops and eagerly loaned her body to mulleted scuzzballs. But she'd never quite rid herself of the cultish hunch that pleasure was sinful, a corruption of the body's true purpose, which was to suffer. Pregnancy had returned her to this hard truth, four times over. She'd grown swollen and pukey. Her nipples had bled. Labor had inflicted a menu of horrors—sadistic contractions, vaginal tears, involuntary pooping—all of which she recalled, somehow, as joyful.

For those keeping score at home, there had been only three labors. Following the birth of our two older boys, Ray had suffered a miscarriage, which had left her gray and hollow-eyed. She had taken this as a definitive sign that, at thirty-five, she could no longer bear children. Thus the twins.

I was sensitive to all this. Ask anyone. During her pregnancies, I had rubbed her feet then quietly latched onto her from behind, a timid satellite tucking my agitated docking device between my legs. Her body, which had never belonged to me, now belonged to children.

Still. There I was, on the Friday night in question, raking my wife's buttocks like a lotto ticket. I gazed with genuine awe upon her lumbar region, the cello swell of her hips.

"Don't get overzealous," she said. "Let me do my thing here."

"Do your thing, and I'll do my thing. Thing One and Thing Two. You bake a cake, and I'll itch on you," I chanted. That's where we were. Dr. Seuss had become part of my game.

"I need my pastry board," Ray announced. She twisted away and began circling the kitchen, gathering up ingredients, while I stood by the island, dumb and obedient as a Labrador.

"It's downstairs. Be a dear and get that for me."

Down I went, into the basement, with its dank caverns of premarital junk, its shitty furnace and slightly less shitty hot water tank, its aspirational anniversary gifts—the massage table! the *Yoga for the Inflexible* DVD!—its whining humidifier and mossy reek of flooded carpeting. I avoided this place. It felt excessively metaphorical.

Some part of me suspected that I'd wind up living down here, once the older two hit puberty and insisted on private rooms in which to stockpile hair gel and chewing gum and dynamite.

I returned to the kitchen with the pastry board on my head and began to emit primitive gibberish intended to convey that I, now a pygmy Sherpa of some sort, had retrieved the desired item for his queen. I guess it bears mentioning that my wife is, like, two inches taller than I am.

Ray responded with her own softer gibberish of gratitude. I laid the pastry board on the kitchen island, and she dumped a cup of white flour onto it and began to hack at a giant cube of butter that advertised itself, implausibly, as grass fed. She folded the butter into the flour with a nonchalance I found enthralling. It was like a marriage. You had these two disparate ingredients that got sort of mashed and pebbled together until, by all appearances, they became a single thing. But you didn't know if the crust was going to crack until you gassed up the oven. And by then, if you think about—which I guess, at that point, I was—it was too late.

"I thought you were doing a cake," I said.

"I'm kind of over cakes."

"Fuck cakes," I agreed. "Too sweet. Too layered. Smug fucking cakes."

Encouragingly, Ray had pulled a bottle of rosé from the fridge and poured a goblet. I took a swig and gargled it like mouthwash.

"I wish you wouldn't do that," Ray said.

"This is how the sommeliers do it in Provence. Or maybe this is how the provincials do it in Somalia."

Ray groaned in that special, long-suffering timbre of hers, and I returned to the sink and finished up every last dish. Then I wiped down the counters and grabbed the hand broom and swept along the baseboards, so as to capture the many particles of food and hair and mouse shit generated by a family of six. I was still very much hoping that my support and consideration in these matters would result in ardent and odiferous kitchen fucking.

Ray began to drip ice water onto her crust with scientific precision. My brother's boyfriend, a Famous Gay Baker out in Sausalito, had showed Ray how to do this once, long ago, when we just had one baby and could travel to other states without a suicide watch.

"Requesting permission to resume itching your Shakespeare," I said. This was a reference to *A Midsummer Night's Dream* and Bottom the Jackass, a role I had played during an unfortunate adolescent community-theater phase. I had confessed this on our first date, and Ray had made a joke, which neither of us could quite remember. It was just another part of the play within a play that marriage becomes.

Ray lifted her neck, the slender tendons flushed a bit with wine. "Permission granted."

"There may be some rubbing involved, too."

"Don't get ahead of yourself."

"What are we thinking in terms of filling?"

"Strawberry. Rhubarb."

"Perfect. The kids will loathe it. They have an instinctual distrust of rhubarb."

"I'm trying to use all the crap in the freezer."

This was aimed at me. I kept a small weed-choked garden in our backyard. Some years ago, I had enjoyed a banner crop of rhubarb, which I had stubbornly incorporated into a variety of inedible cobblers and smoothies before cramming the balance in deep freeze.

"Hands off, Romeo. I need to chill this." Ray popped the crust in the freezer and emerged with plastic take-out containers full of petrified rhubarb. For a while there, we both worked diligently. She chopped. I scratched. The house breathed quietly. Ray kept at her wine with sips that called to mind a fairy-tale queen drinking a potion.

"I know what you're up to," she said.

I said nothing. Nothing was my big play here, silence and gesture. I lifted her shirt, and her skin was a pallid veldt with lavish constellations of freckle. I kissed each tiny blemish.

"Remember Ryan," Ray said quietly.

I hummed. Our second oldest had been fascinated by these birthmarks as a child. He'd spent hours tracing the lines between them with his pointer finger. Deathmarks, he called them, and we eventually stopped correcting him. Kids know the score.

Once, while Ray was off at one of her techno torture classes, I'd plunked the older boys down in front of a documentary on mass-extinction events. Meteors. Plagues. Oceans rancid with sulfuric acid, plumes of volcanic ash. Ray had come home to a barrage of teary questions involving rotting dinosaurs and whether it was true that the sun was going to swallow the earth.

"I was trying to put things in perspective for them," I explained.

"How is presenting images of Auschwitz in any way putting things *in perspective* for your children?" Her cheeks were the color of tartare. "They're still babies, you shithead."

I apologized, of course. The Shithead always apologized. It was the Shithead's one redeeming quality. But the Holocaust stuff was pretty tasteful overall. And I sort of believed what I'd told her. Evolution had hardwired the death instinct into our species. It was what allowed us to appreciate being alive, to take joy in our infinitesimal span within the cosmic story.

So maybe I was feeling lucky, on that particular night, in the grander scheme of things. I plucked Ray's elastic waistband and tugged questioningly downward.

"Don't look at my ass," she said faintly. "I know you're looking at it." She began decapitating strawberries. I began to knead her cheeks, and Ray emitted a growl of reluctant pleasure. It was dark enough now that I could see her face in the reflection of the window. I kissed her neck some more and said a few things, almost all true, about her beauty and grace. Then she was done with the strawberries. "Get me the dough, little Bottom," she said. "And the rolling pin."

I approved of these orders, the winking innuendo of them. I didn't even mind the sobriquet. A small man gets used to such minor humiliations. We listen for intent, not content.

Ray took the rolling pin and gingerly thinned the crust. You didn't want to handle it too much, the Famous Gay Baker said during his tutorial, or the butter wouldn't ejaculate properly. I believe that was how he phrased it. Then he and my wife howled with glee and molested one another in a very nonsexual manner.

Ray draped the crust onto a Pyrex. I continued scratching with one hand while, with the other, I reached for the canola oil. This all had to be done quietly, efficiently. I kissed behind her ears while twisting the top off.

"I need to zest a lemon."

"Do that," I said. "Zest a lemon. Use *zest* as a verb. It's filthy sounding."

I poured oil on my wife's pendulous posterior and made the whole muscular operation quite sleek. I eased into the spot at the base of her spine, where the coccyx lay nestled. If I could linger here, there was some chance she would lose her bearings. But I couldn't be in a hurry. No, a hurry would not do. Ray was thirty-eight. Already her body seemed to be yearning for the hormonal hibernation of menopause, losing moisture, losing heat. I, on the other hand, had somewhat regressed. The masturbation I have alluded to. But I also had a hard time pacing myself, which was a big problem, given the rarity of copulative events, our proven fertility, and our many preexisting children. What I needed was some kind of miniature stun gun. That and patience.

"I should crisp up the crust," Ray murmured. "It'll wind up sludgy if I don't."

"Right. But what if we just let the oven preheat a bit longer? No harm in that, darling. How many years have we got before the knee braces and colostomy bags?"

Ray stiffened.

"I just mean that we have to seize life," I whispered, changing course, possibly into the realm of soda pop slogans. "We have to be grateful for everything we have, the kids, our house, this miraculous body. I still dream about you."

Ray snorted. "What do you dream about?"

"Ireland. Green fields. Those low stonewalls. Sheep."

"So basically a poster of Ireland."

"No. Us. Driving some little European sedan, stopping at quaint inns along the coast and taking long walks at dusk. Big greasy meals. Hot baths. A few books we never get around to reading. Sleeping in."

"Are you taking off your pants, Jake? Is that what's happening back there?"

I continued to massage my wife's backside and now brought her hips into the action. Ray had a bum hip from back in her field hockey days, bone spurs or something, and I knew where she liked me to press, which was maybe another thing you could say about marriage: for better or worse, you knew where to press.

"I know," I said softly, half to myself. "You're tired. Of course you are. You work hard. I'm not blind. I understand how lucky I am. A woman like you. I wish you could see how beautiful you look."

There was no chance this was going to work. It was Little Bighorn, Gallipoli, the Charge of the Light Brigade. Then again, why take the colonial view on things? I slid my hands along the striated muscles that flanked Ray's spine. I heard a clink and glanced up to see that my wife had set aside her lemon. Her eyes were closed. A yellow dust like pollen lay all around the grater.

"The oven," she moaned.

"Let me handle that. You stay put."

"It does feel good."

Jake be nimble. Jake be quick. "That was easy, no?"

"Your hands got warm."

"They did."

Then, by God, my wife did something unthinkable, unprecedented, unsanitary. She dropped her forearms onto that fruit-spattered island and bent over in such a manner that the cleavage of her buttocks nestled itself against my pleading pulse. And I, your hero, your dainty Jake, stood taking all this in, the husband now a statue of gratitude, the mingling of our pubic kink tickling splendidly, the greedy vasculature of my erection fully athrob.

My first impulse was to drop to my knees. My second impulse was to fetch a cell phone. Ray reached back and took hold of my wrist, to show me her condition. She was wet—significantly damp, anyway. "You feel that?" I heard her say, from far above. "You want that, little man?"

"Yuh," I said.

I wasn't sure what to do, though. As far as I'd thought this through, I imagined we'd wind up on the floor, with a few strategic oven mitts scattered to keep our brittle bones from bruising. But Ray wanted me inside now. I wanted that, too. It was only my wife's long and sturdy legs that presented a problem. How to say this delicately? We were not ... vertically aligned. A phone book would have helped, or a small but tasteful hydraulic jack. Instead, I grabbed my wife's shoulders and sort of leaped myself inside her.

This was what I'd wanted, the rut and rampage of the thing, the doggy style with the human brain, and I concentrated, in those initial seconds, on not looking down at the pungent undulations of Ray's gluteal region. "Should we?" she rasped. "I mean. The kids. Okay. All right, then. Yeah. Like that. No, like before. Like before but slower."

So we proceeded, with a lot of fiercely puffed stage direction and me trying to keep up, keep in, keep going. I rose onto my tippy toes and let her hips hoist me aloft on the upswing. It was like being at zero gravity. I thought of the tagline from a horror movie that had haunted my youth. *In space, no one can hear you fuck.* Perhaps I was misremembering.

On restless nights, hounded by some insomniac tenant, I wandered into my children's rooms and stared at their faces.

Sleep suspended them in stillness. But they were in space, too, tumbling through private galaxies of dreams, solemn pilgrims in a universe of wishes and fears and symbols. Only in waking would they begin anew the human project of living and dying.

Why was I thinking about any of this?

My wife's back was shimmering beneath me like a pelt. The scent rising from her gyrating derriere was intoxicating, germy, like a sneeze onto the forearm. I watched in rapture as Ray curled a shy hand around her hip and flicked herself with stirring precision.

But somehow it was going wrong. My end of it, I mean. Rather than feeling as I expected—ecstatic and tensile—I was tumbling from the grip of desire. Ray bent her knees to bid me greater purchase, and her thighs trembled magnificently. But dainty Jake had gone numb. Though his body was there—stubbornly flopping, making pet noises—his spirit had spun off, a moon devoured by the lust of his given star. "Go," Ray said. "Go go go. Yuh-yuh-yuh."

I could neither *go* nor *yuh*, for I had turned to taffy inside my beloved.

Ray cast a confused look over her shoulder. Then she reached back to investigate the situation, and her eyes flashed pity. Whatever else might be said about me as a spouse—self-involved, impatient, moody, callous, well, that was a start—I'd been reliable in the boner department.

With a generous jigger of oil and plenty of elbow grease, Ray returned me to readiness. Off we went. "Good, Jake. Fuck me like that. Fuck me just like that. Are you going to come all over my ass? Come all over my ass!"

How grateful I was for these exhortations! It was the tone, I believe, that undid me, a dire enthusiasm I associated with the Special Olympics. So then I was on to that, the mentally handicapped, the grinning gimps in their ill-fitting shorts, and out I slipped again, like something extruded.

A third effort, which involved shortening, I refuse to revisit.

For a minute or so we stood not saying anything. Ray pulled up her pajama bottoms and gave me an awful hug. "That was fun," she said. My eyes kept settling on the strawberries she had cut for the filling, bloody and succulent in a glass measuring cup.

"Please don't," I said.

"It was," she said more softly.

The oven beeped and Ray stepped back, and I retreated to our bedroom to sulk. I felt like one of the lesser deities from mythology, Limpos, God of Wounded Masculinity. Mainly, I was furious at myself. I'd worked so hard to entice Ray, to bring her into my drooling diorama. Maybe that was the problem—I'd exhausted my desire. Or perhaps my vas deferens had become occluded with pornographic gunk. What did it matter?

I could hear Ray in the kitchen, tending to her pie. I hated her for a few pleasing minutes: her unreasonable height, her listless libido, the power she held over me. This would be another rift between us, another thing to make me frantic and needy while my wife went about her business of never having sex with me in the kitchen again because I'd whiskey-dicked the whole shebang. I thought about marching back into that kitchen and finishing what I'd started. But my wee cock had withdrawn into its sad scrotal cell.

I closed my eyes and started to cry a little. My kids suddenly appeared, floating around me in silver space suits. Through a series of porthole windows, the black depths of heaven hurtled by. Then the ship lurched and began to come apart, and I opened my eyes to find Ray perched on the edge of the bed.

"What time is it?"

"Midnight."

She laid the back of her hand on my forehead. "You fell asleep."

"How'd the pie turn out?"

She made a face. "Rhubarb doesn't defrost especially well."

"Sorry about that," I said.

"Don't beat yourself up," she said. "You tried."

"Some try."

"You wanted things to go a certain way," she said carefully.

"You were *ready*," I said.

Ray shrugged, a tad sheepishly, and avoided meeting my eye.

"Wait a second," I said. "You weren't faking it in there, were you?"

Ray let out a long, dramatic breath—half Lamaze, half rosé. "Maybe embellishing a little."

"Oh Christ," I said.

"You told me to be honest."

"The perfect end to a romantic evening," I said.

Ray leaned down and brought her face so close to mine I could see nothing but her weary eyes. "I can't *use* romantic," she said. "It's lovely but inessential, like confetti. This is our life now, Jacob. You put a bunch of babies in me. We have a mortgage. You provide a steady income. You help with the kids. I'm grateful for that."

"So what? I get a passing grade?" I said.

"I love you. That's what I'm telling you. That's what's happening here." She kissed me on the mouth, somewhat defiantly. Then she sat up and disappeared into our kitchen and returned with the pie. She stood at the foot of the bed and held the pie aloft, her body weaving in the light from the hall, and much drunker than I'd realized.

"What are you doing?"

Without a word, Ray flipped the pie over onto the bed. It made a wet sucking noise.

For a second, neither one of us could believe she'd done it. We stood staring at the glistening innards, maroon and somewhat placental frankly.

Maybe this was marriage, too. The boiled mess of it, the bizarre sacrificial gestures of devotion and wrath, the lattice design, so carefully prepared to suggest domestic harmony, only to be desecrated by incoherent hungers.

Ray reached down and scooped up a large shard of crust. Her voice sang out in rhapsody. "The course of true love never did run smooth." On all fours she crawled toward me, naked, as beautiful as Eve and wasted to the point of innocence. Steam rose from the slurry fruit and filled the small red chamber around us. "Open up now, little Bottom. Let mama fuck you silly with this pie."

SING A SONG OF SIXPENCE

SAMUEL LIGON

THE MAID'S NOSE WAS snipped off by a blackbird while she was hanging clothes in the garden. I didn't see it, having just walked away from the window upstairs, but there were plenty of witnesses, and while one claimed her nose was pecked off, and another claimed it was snapped off, and the maid herself, before bleeding to death, said it had definitely been snipped off, the essence of the thing remained the same. My beautiful Tammy was attacked by a blackbird while hanging laundry in the garden. This was after the pie was opened, after the king had turned to the bottle, and the queen to one of her young lovers. It was a pattern with them, part of the reason for all the laundry—the king soiling his robes and pantaloons, the queen bingeing and purging and fornicating all over the castle. They were horrible people, the king and queen. What do you expect? Treat people like gods, and they'll behave like swine. But I'm talking about Tammy here, my one true love, disfigured and wailing out in the garden.

Had the physician been able to stop her bleeding, I'd have gone on loving Tammy, with or without a nose. Without eyes, I'd have loved her. Without ears or a chin, ankles or elbows, propped on a straw bed for three and ninety years, I'd have worshipped Tammy. Had an eagle swooped down and pecked off her buttocks, severing her legs and causing them to fall from her body, I'd have braved fire, eaten rocks, tamed demons for the love of Tammy's torso. Had she but lived.

The king was in the counting house, counting out his money. Do you see what I'm saying about these people? The king had a separate building for his plunder, brick and stone, while the rest of us lived in mud-daubed hovels. He kept a flask in his robes filled with rye, and I'd hear him grunting and muttering drunkenly in the counting house as he slobbered over his gold.

The queen was in the parlor, eating bread and honey. She could never get enough, and after she ate, she purged, and after she purged, she'd slather one of her boys with lard or butter, or wrap him in a string of sausages for more bingeing. Sometimes she'd nip at a finger or toe, but she hadn't started eating her lovers yet. Not in earnest. The way she examined their haunches, though, poking and prodding, you knew it was only a matter of time. This is what I mean about these people, why somebody had to stop them.

It took two years to train the birds. Tammy thought we should use poison, but I wanted drama, the bold statement. "Jackdaws, then," she said. "Or ravens. The ghosts of the murdered dead to peck out their eyes." But it was blackbirds I wanted, the sweetness of their song. I did what I did for love, for Tammy. I did what I did for hatred, too. I did what I did as the one grand gesture of my life.

"Poetry must have something in it barbaric, vast, and wild," Tammy would say to me, quoting Diderot, as we lay on our bed of dung, happy in spite of our loathing for our lords and ladies. I'd quote Diderot right back to her: "Hang the last king by the guts of the last priest," and we'd make wild pagan love until morning. Say what you will about bile and simmering rage, but our hatred for our betters bound us as much as anything. I loved Tammy for the murder in her heart as much as for her club foot or cleft palate. We were the ones who should have been royal—or so much more than royal—not a baker and scullery maid but gods, wrathful and glorious, emerging from the sun dripping fire.

When the pie was opened, the birds began to sing, one tentative whistle and then another and then a keening chorus as they came to life inside the vented crust. The flurry that followed was the most startling thing I've ever witnessed, all my dreams of murder come to life on explosive black wings. I thought of Diderot's words, "Only great passions can elevate the soul to great things." I thought of Tammy in the garden, waiting for night, our furious love and hatred, our plotting and scheming, training those birds, and now the magic of their rising on wafts of steam, a flurry of feather and birdsong and gasps from the royal fuckfaces as the birds prepared to peck through their eyes and into their worm-infested brains. The glory of it all.

But those fucking birds. Do you know what they did? They flew straight up and out the windows. That's what they did.

After all that shrieking and flapping, the air fairly crackled. How horribly wrong it had all gone. Instead of a new life for Tammy and me, I would be led to the block for beheading, or more likely, I'd be disemboweled, then beheaded, and finally quartered, while Tammy would go on without me, quoting Diderot to somebody else.

The king hit his flask. "Nicely done," he said to me. "Jim, is it?"

I looked up from the floor. "Bob," I said.

"Bravo, Bob," the king said, toasting me with his flask before taking another long pull.

"Wasn't that a dainty dish," the queen said, reaching for the pie pan and stuffing her gob with fistfuls of bird shit and crumbling crust.

"Come on, Elizabeth," the king said. "We're not supposed to eat that."

"Of course we're supposed to eat it," the queen said.

"I'm going to the counting house," the king said, but the queen ignored him. I walked to the window and saw my Tammy in the garden below. The queen filled her pie hole. Maybe we'd find another way to set ourselves free. Outside, the blackbirds wheeled against a perfect blue sky. One pulled away from the others and circled on extended wings, drifting slowly, silently, down, down, down.

THE CARRIE NATION

Like so many great Americans, Carrie Nation was blessed with visions from God. Like so many great Americans, she embraced a kind of creative destruction. God told Carrie to throw things, to smash things, to break things, which Carrie did. She was a smasher. A crasher. She was also opposed to tight clothing, refusing to wear a corset. She is the mother of attacking bars with a hatchet.

MAKES 2 COCKTAILS

1 corset
1 cast-iron skillet
1 hand organ
1 beer
Handfuls of durian fruit, dragon fruit, loganberry, saffron, rambutan, ripe jackfruit, guava leaf, lemongrass, devil's horsewhip, tamarind, arrowroot, tonka bean, sapodilla

6 bottles Chartreuse Vieillissement Exceptionnellement Prolongé
6 bottles 1778 Clos de Griffier Vieux Cognac
6 bottles St-Germain
Whiskey
Sweet vermouth
Bitters
2 cherries

Rage
1 hatchet
1 heavy rock

1   Set the oven to broil. Take off your corset. It's uncomfortable, constricting, and bad for your vital organs. Place it in the cast-iron skillet. Place the cast-iron skillet in the oven and forget about it. Now that you can breathe again, take up your hand organ and sing five hymns. Drink the beer. Muddle the ingredients you've gathered in handfuls. On the kitchen table, place the bottles of Chartreuse, Cognac, and St-Germain. Make a Manhattan. I usually use bourbon, but you can also use rye. People in Wisconsin use brandy. No one

CONTINUED

knows why. Some people insist a Manhattan must be served up. These insufferables must be driven back to Portland. But you don't have time for that. Take a deep breath. Tap into your rage. Gulp at your drink. Heft your hatchet. Destroy everything on the table, reveling in the smashing glass, the liquor perfume, the dangerous booze slick all over the tile. Sip your drink. Throw a rock through the window over the sink. Throw away what you've muddled. The muddling was only to occupy your wicked, idle hands.

MOTHERFUCKING STRAWBERRY RHUBARB PIE

Home-frozen strawberries and rhubarb both get soggy when thawed if you don't take extra precautions. I say home-frozen, because flash-frozen fruit tends to behave pretty well regardless of whether it has been thawed or not, maybe because it was frozen so quickly the water in its cells didn't burst its cell walls, so as it bakes it holds its water better. DIY frozen fruit won't be as easy to bake with as flash frozen, but it's still perfectly good and delicious, so don't be shy about using it. First, thaw home-frozen rhubarb and strawberries in a colander and discard the juice. Then add the fruit to the recipe as directed. You'll probably end up using more fruit (by weight, not volume), since it will be deflated compared to fresh or flash-frozen fruit. The texture will be slightly different—a little more solid than fresh or flash-frozen pie fruit would have been—but it won't swamp your pie with juice. That's the important part.

MAKES 1 PIE

1 recipe Pie School Pastry
  Crust (see page 241)
2½ cups (about ⅘ pound)
  fresh or frozen rhubarb,
  sliced ½-inch thick
2½ cups (1 heaping pint)
  fresh or frozen strawberries

1 cup granulated sugar
Juice of 1 medium lemon
  (about 1½ tablespoons)
Pinch ground nutmeg
Pinch kosher salt
5 tablespoons all-purpose
  flour

2 tablespoons chilled unsalted
  butter, cut into small chunks
Egg-white wash (1 egg white
  beaten with 1 teaspoon
  water)
Demerara sugar, for sprinkling

CONTINUED

1   Prepare the dough and refrigerate it for at least 1 hour or overnight.

2   Roll out the bottom crust on a floured surface and place it in a 9- or 10-inch pie plate. (To make sure the plate is the right size, pile the fruit into the bare plate, let it reach the height of the rim of the plate but do not let it go over, put that fruit in your mixing bowl, wipe out your pie plate, and continue with the recipe.) Tuck the crust into the plate and trim the edges. Refrigerate the crust while you prepare the next steps of the recipe.

3   Preheat the oven to 425 degrees F.

4   In a large bowl, mix the rhubarb with the strawberries, granulated sugar, lemon juice, nutmeg, and salt. Taste and adjust the flavors as needed. Stir in the flour and butter and set aside.

5   Roll out the top crust on a floured surface and then retrieve the pie plate from the refrigerator.

6   Pour the filling into the bottom crust, mound it with your hands, and drape the top crust over it. Trim, fold, and flute the edges. Cut generous steam vents, brush the top crust with the egg-white wash, and sprinkle it with the Demerara sugar.

7   Bake the pie in the middle of the oven for 10 to 15 minutes or until the crust is blond and blistered. Rotate the pie front to back and then reduce the heat to 375 degrees F. Bake about 40 to 50 minutes more, until the crust is golden brown and the juices are thickened and bubble slowly through the vents.

8   Cool the pie on a wire rack for at least 1 hour. Serve warm or at room temperature. Store leftovers on the kitchen counter, loosely wrapped in a towel, for up to 3 days.

*After Mother
died her red
dress continued
baking pies*

—C. A. CONRAD, *THE BOOK OF FRANK*

MOTHER'S RED DRESS ENTERS A PIE IN THE COUNTY FAIR

ALEXANDRA TEAGUE

The living think they know everything
about heartbeats—hutches of rabbits

with their prizewinning ears twitching
at rumors of themselves, bottle-fed pigs

suckling now at the bright night air—
all life's straw-stink and cage made safer

with ruffled ribbons and turned-over fear
as the Moonraker's one long arm hovers

in high copper sky before plunging. The living
scream as if the heart is a basket, though no one

falls out. They tuck the cherries into fluting
lattice nests, seal the jelly's glow: even, crystalline

as cathedral glass. They don't see a woman's
dress is just her heart beating crisscrossing

gingham and stitch: the hem fraying past skin,
more unravel than red, more Red Beauty

than fabric. They don't see the trees growing
up from glass pans—crumbling buttery crusts

with their branches. The sweetest glowing
peaches seep the oven floor. The living put

mystics into Ball jars: add pectin to set god
into flesh. Santa Rosa scouring her lovely face

with pepper and lye to end attraction—to shut
desire down like an electric ride. As if any place

can't become a fair—light spilling over fields
as the judges close their eyes to taste:

noting *lemon* for *infinite*. *Nutmeg* for *unreal,
unknowable*. They eat apple and crust as if it were

more delicious than their own hunger.

PIE AND WHISKEY

KIM BARNES

JUNE IN MONTANA, and Duff Finnegan sits in front of his woodstove, listening to opera on his beloved hi-fi. He's kicked off his Romeos and wears only socks, pushed down until they flag from his toes. He pulls his cap lower, shrugs up his collar. Like some old woman, he thinks, hot on one end, cold on the other. In another five minutes, it might reverse, and he'll be draping the quilt over his legs, tearing off the hat because his scalp has burst into flames. He blames the aging furnace and prefers the honest pop of the fire, but he knows that there is no getting over old age.

He pats his left shirt pocket. Empty. Why anyone gives a damn about an old man and his cigarettes, he doesn't know, but his daughter, Annie, has gathered them up and taken them away, along with the butter and all the salt in the house. Except for the two fingers of whiskey she allows him each night, all of his pleasures are gone.

He feels the heat come into his feet, their temperature rising with the voice of a then young Enrico Caruso. Duff remembers coming home from the war, back when he could have all the cigarettes and salt he wanted. He'd been in Madison, visiting his navy buddy Gil, when he met Claudia at the skating rink. She was buxom, a little brassy, a fine-looking girl, but he was already in love, not with another woman but with the opera that he and Gil listened to on the shortwave as they lay in their racks, bound for Korea. Duff had gone into the service a bow-legged kid with jug ears and an eighth-grade education. Three years later, he came home two inches taller, twenty pounds heavier, with a heart that was aching for arias. It may have been the very thing that drew Claudia to him—why else would a college girl date a hick from the sticks?—but it wasn't a fondness you shared with just anyone. Over the years, he's been given plenty of hell for nestling his ear up against the radio. But who's alive to give him hell now? Ron Brewster, Ted Johnson, Merle Trigsted—every man on his logging crew dead except him.

Duff holds his breath a moment to better hear the tenderness in Caruso's tenor, the fragility barely contained. Not a weakness but a vulnerability, a timbre that would darken as he aged. Duff has never had much chance to argue with anybody about opera, but if he had to defend Caruso, he'd say that he felt more human in his presence—not transported, just human.

Duff groans himself up and checks the thermostat. Too hot to be healthy, his wife would have said. She'd kept their bedroom window cracked no matter the season. He misses the cold on his face, the warmth of her tucked up against him. "You're a pathetic son of a bitch," he says aloud and makes his way to the kitchen, not because he is hungry but because he knows he should eat before he takes the whiskey, and it's the whiskey that he wants. The refrigerator is bare except for a carton of Egg Beaters, a brick of low-fat cheese—rations from Annie's monthly run to Costco. In the freezer, nothing but a bag of mixed vegetables, which, if he had salt, he might choke down. He takes out the package, dumps two fistfuls into a cast-iron skillet, sees the sink full of water, and that's when he remembers the roast

Annie had left to thaw. He mustn't forget, she'd said. She didn't need him poisoning his fool self on top of everything else. He dips his hand, brings up the meat, its deep-red marbling leeched pink. How long has it been here? Hours? A day?

He presses his thumbs into the roast, feels it give like wet cotton. He brings it to his nose, sniffs, smells the blood gone sour. When he looks up, he sees his reflection in the window: his white hair fanned from his head, the gruesome bundle in his hands like the body of a newborn.

For a moment, the image stuns him into stillness, but then he takes a step back, cocks his arm, and pitches the roast at the window. The glass doesn't shatter, exactly. For the most part, its pane remains intact, except for the football-size hole through its center. Duff peers at it with some wonder. He didn't know he still had it in him.

The breeze comes in cool and easy, just right. He looks at his hands, wipes them dry, sees the pecan pie Annie left—his favorite. Only one thin sliver each evening, she'd warned—his heart couldn't take much more. He cuts a thick wedge, then moves to the high cupboard where's she's pushed back the liquor, pours a deep shot. He takes his glass and plate, goes to the hi-fi, and settles the needle. He eases down into his chair, cuts the end from the piece of pie, pushes it aside, then rotates his plate three times. The tip, he'll save for last and whatever luck is still left him. He lifts his glass as Caruso's voice fills the room.

"To you, my friend," he says, and takes the whiskey in one swallow, although, more than anything, he had wanted it to last.

YOUR FRIENDS WON'T VISIT YOU WHEN YOU MOVE <u>TO THE</u> COUNTRY

DEVIN BECKER

Although that's why you moved there.
You thought, going through your soon-to-be
country home, "My friends will love coming here.
We'll sit outside, drink whiskey
at the picnic table until the wee."

But the country is hard and you won't
even see the wee anymore, except
those nights when the baby you had
(because what else does one do in the country
besides breed) wakes up in the middle of it.

                  Where you live
is too far. And the parties and bars
are all in town, with your friends,

who don't want to stay in your weird
barn apartment, or if they do stay, once,
because they feel bad for you,
their skin will erupt
in an earwig-induced plague
or else they'll wake terrified by the coyotes'
howls or the cows' lows.

And cows do low, and sound terrifying
when you're all alone and your wife's
asleep and all you can hear is the rumble
they make, those huge, dumb beasts
not fifty feet from where you sit
wedged between your ever-
increasing-in-size dog and the couch's armrest,
which is your spot, you realize, the one
you keep indenting and indenting to where
no one else feels comfortable
sitting there anymore, and so even
when you do get them out, these
"friends," to the country where you live with
cows and shit and bugs
and the family you *do* love,
who you would do anything for
(like move to the country)
your friends say, "Wow
we should be—" "Man,
what time is it—" "Whoa,
we've got Pilates in the morning . . ."

And you hate your friends
but you love them and the late-night

impromptu Boggle tournaments
they can't stop
posting about on the internet,
and so you drink so much whiskey,
alone, watching the cows outside
move their mud about,
that you fall in love
with the skittish one, the poop-
brown one who runs when you're nearby
and you say, no, no, you're
my friend, come here, poop cow.

And you watch the moon,
you see the light shifting
afternoon to afternoon
almost imperceptibly
as the spherical nature
of the earth becomes
more and more apparent,
and the smells sweeten:
woodsmoke and dull, muddled
shit, and pine needles in sun,
and gravel after the rain
and hail, which smells
like gravel, and wind,
which smells like it could pull
the footing out from under you.

AND THEN THERE WAS RUM CAKE

NINA MUKERJEE FURSTENAU

I.

"WE USED TO WANT WHISKEY," Dorsey said like a gunslinger, his mouth twisted with one lip edged up, "when us kids were about fifteen." I try to picture this word, *whiskey*, erupting out of him at fifteen when Dorsey was a skinny farm boy. In a photo from 1942 he was dressed in baggy overalls and scuffed, round-toed boots. There may have been a cowlick.

"We'd go to Schmonig's drugstore to see Big Ed; he weighed about 440 pounds and waddled around like a big duck. 'Ed, I'd like a pint,' I'd say, handing him two bucks. He'd say to look in the garbage can out behind after a while."

The boys found the whiskey, Dorsey told me, and would drink and ride around in an early 1930s Chevy on gravel roads, some of them standing on the running boards, some inside the car. They would jump off into fields strewn with corn stubble or lush with green stalks, depending on the time of year, to pee, whooping as they ran back.

"That old bohemian Ed Schmonig," Dorsey murmured. "He went on a diet and went down to 220 pounds, then he went back to eating again, had a stroke, and died."

I maneuvered the car into a parking space by the clinic doors as Dorsey talked. When I turned the ignition off, Dorsey didn't seem to notice. His eyes, usually inquisitive and hopeful, might have been sad, but I couldn't catch them as they slid to the side and off into the distance.

I'd first met Dorsey nearly eighteen years before this moment in the car. I was twenty-one, getting ready to marry his son, Terry, and Dorsey had wanted me to feel at home in his earth-contact house nestled into the Missouri hills. From the living room I couldn't tell that three exterior walls of the house were buried up to the rafters in the hill. A window-filled front wall opened to sloping land where a horde of chickens, ducks, and sheep milled around waiting to follow Dorsey whenever they could. It was unlike the clipped lawn of my parents' yellow ranch house in small-town Kansas, but more than that, it had nothing in common with my Northern Indian roots. I had no vocabulary for farm life. Dorsey looked me squarely in the eyes with kindness.

First, though, he shoved logs into his woodstove and asked about my Indian church. He didn't know the word for temple. At twenty-one, I avoided talking about religion because I could never seem to answer in simple sentences. My Kansas friends, weaned on a clear and straightforward story of Christ and his father, couldn't grasp that one story was never enough for Indians. We had hundreds, it seemed to me, and I did not know them. Each time someone asked me about religion in school, it felt like a taunt. And it was, once or twice: *You worship cows.* Anger, mostly at myself for not knowing what to say, made me clench my fists and keep my story private.

"I like churches," I said carefully. "They're beautiful, but I have never attended one." When Dorsey looked into the distance, my heart sank a little.

"You worship cows," he said, and a sweet, openhearted expression came into his eyes. Even as I began to respond, I realized I could not condense a five-thousand-year-old religion into terms he would understand.

"It's more about respecting all forms of life," I said.

Dorsey considered the log in his hands and shoved it into the stove. He straightened, glanced outside at his cows in the distance, the sheep in the door of the barn, the ducks and chickens near the window, and nodded with a slight smile. I would always love that he distilled my world into something he could relate to with one sweeping look and nod.

Eighteen years later, when Dorsey was seventy-one, his kidneys in ruins from diabetes, I helped out by taking him to the clinic. That day, as we sat in the car, engine clicking, his door opened from the outside and my sister-in-law, Susie, stood there.

"Hey, Dad."

When I walked around the car, I could see her heels making little indents in the hot tarmac beside the car. "He's been telling me about his dead friends," I said when I reached Susie's shoulder. She sighed. Lately there had been a lot of stories about the boys who used to get whiskey from Big Ed. Dead Eye Chelly—he'd had a car accident and his left eye hung a little; he could see out of it, though—got drunk, walked onto a freeway in California, and got run over. Goofy Gus died of stomach cancer. Gene Tackner died in a mental hospital. Harry Bunn died of a heart attack. Bull Neilson was the only one still alive. Their deaths weighed on Dorsey as his illness advanced, and I sat, sometimes for hours, listening to his stories, letting him sort through it all.

"Well, I guess maybe I don't really need this, Suz." Dorsey lifted his right knee by using both hands under the kneecap and put his foot down on the pavement. I grabbed his canes from the back seat and stood ready.

"Let's see what it's like, Dad," Susie said and started walking slowly as she talked. "They say you'll feel better because your blood will be clean." I walked behind them, leaning forward, ready to help should Dorsey stumble.

In the clinic, Papa looked smaller as he sat in a vinyl chair. The other patients were talking. They came three times a week and knew each other. Dorsey looked away from them as he walked into the consultation room alone. I envisioned a young doctor with a confident handshake explaining procedures while a nurse hooked up a machine. Dorsey would be with the others next time, he would have said. It was going to be all right, he would have murmured. I envisioned a man in a lab coat patting Dorsey on the head. My stomach rolled a little at the thought of his skin pierced by equipment.

Through the walls, I felt Dorsey squint at me, and his smile pulled up one edge of his lips.

II.

I, too, needed gunslinger swagger, or at least that snicker when I walked into Dorsey's mother's funeral with store-bought crust. I was twenty-four, had married Terry two years earlier, and was just meeting our Nebraska relatives. My new clan was gathered in the basement of a small church in Fremont. The steps downstairs were linoleum covered with metal edges stapled to each step, making it easy to hear people approach.

I held two brown-sugar apple pies. By some miracle, the golden-brown crust had stayed lofty and beautifully mounded. The tops glistened with the crystals of turbinado sugar I had sprinkled over them to cloak the fact that the crust was from the grocery's refrigerated aisle. The slits in the top crusts made you want to lean into the aroma, American and lusty, sweet and comforting.

The crusts made it look like I knew what I was doing.

There was a brief pause as the Nebraska women cast their eyes upon the pies. I slid them onto the table, which was laden with other fare—brisket, dinner rolls, seven-layer salad with peas and bacon pieces, Jell-O salads, cakes, and pies of lesser height. My pies looked comfortable there. I slid away to stand at Terry's elbow.

I was living a pie lie.

Although I was a Southeast Kansas girl—riding my ten-speed bike over mimosa flowers crushed on the hot asphalt roads, playing softball, craving sweet cherry Slurpees from 7-Eleven—inside our house no one made pies. Or mashed potatoes. Or roasted brisket. There was chickpea flour (*baeshun*) in the cupboard, and you had to rummage for all-purpose white. When I pulled the white ten-pound bag from the back of the cupboard to make a cake or muffins, it scraped over the yellowish baeshun perpetually in a fine layer on the shelf. Chicken curry, *chatni*, *piash*, and sometimes pakoras made of spinach or onions mixed in baeshun batter and fried—these were the foods that ruled my mother's kitchen. I learned pie baking in seventh-grade home economics class. That same year, I started making mashed potatoes and gravy as a side dish for some of our dinners, another gift of the Lakeside Junior High curriculum.

In the church basement, Cousin Mary said the crust was amazing. She mentioned its beauty, its perfectly mounded robustness, its golden-sparkling glory. I fidgeted. In Southern Kansas, standing out was not encouraged. The trouble was, no matter what, I was different than the Susies and Joes with their entire family story and church preference understood, their cousins that worked at the movie theater and grocery store, and their ties to the region securely in place. With blue-black unruly hair and an untold story, I would never be seamless in my community.

I did not always mind this. Our family club was comforting. When I stood wide-eyed and didn't respond, Cousin Mary mentioned the pie crusts again, louder this time.

I roused myself.

"Really, it's the filling with the flavor," I said as mildly as I could.

But something about my unease had surfaced. It was crust-induced guilt, plain and simple. Despite the fact that the brown sugar and green apple combination made a fine, tasty-on-the-tongue, exceptional pie, it felt as if there were a red light flashing over my head. The family milling around the table glanced over their shoulders at me, eyebrows raised, no doubt because of the red miasma of shame above my forehead. Then their eyes dropped to the pies. I was about to learn that if you want to blend in, do not bring beautiful pie.

"Amazing crust," someone said as they passed with a kind smile.

"It's the brown sugar," I tried again, desperate. "It's a Missouri recipe, that filling."

The tide did not turn.

"But that crust," the women cajoled, admiring my effort. They wanted me to belong.

"Hope there's a piece left," Cousin Diane said. "That crust, um-hum."

I could make pie crust and, in fact, often did. But in a borrowed Nebraska kitchen, expediency had been the goal. I wanted to laugh off the imposter crust with a casual "Me and the Safeway crust-makers"—entwined fingers here—"we're like this." I would have capped it off with a chuckle: "Ha! Ha!"

But it was too late to come clean. I had wanted to contribute as a supporting cast member who didn't draw attention to herself, but this fake crust had failed me. I could have joined the ever-tantalizing circle of Women Who Bake in the family, yet there was a part of me that was glad to not be absorbed.

"It ain't all pie in the sky, I'll tell you that."

Driving back from the clinic visit, Dorsey fell silent for a minute. That day, after hours of dialysis, he wasn't remembering lighthearted days. He talked about his brother Duane and the war years. He was irritated at something his wife told him.

"Ruth's church says something that isn't true, I think. They say when you die you don't have no face. But I think your soul gotta have a face on it or else how are you going to recognize people? Hell, that's eternity we're talking about with no face at all."

"I don't know," I began, sensing this was about Dorsey really, about finding his people and belonging to a group in the afterlife when the time came, soon now.

I considered my family's view of death. In Northern India, if you connected to the grace in all things, your soul went back at death to Atman, or the great soul, in a sort of boundless soul soup. Surface identity didn't play into things. On the plus side, you knew without doubt your place in relation to infinity. But for Dorsey, I suspected this would not be comforting. I kept quiet.

I was raised thinking it wasn't considerate to put ideas out in the world that conflicted too much with others', that to make people uncomfortable was bad manners. For the first time, I saw this conduct had not served me well. The work of being visible was hard for me, and still is today, nearly seventeen years after Dorsey's death. My core fear, I see now, was of not belonging should I speak my mind. To me, the world was made up of multiple and equally valid ways to reach God, and equally valid ways to live, but this felt beyond the pale in Southern Kansas.

Because it never occurred to Dorsey to prevaricate on differences, I could see his imperfections and confusions were not so different from my own. I loved him for that. What he wanted was to seamlessly belong to community in death. He wanted to know people there, see their faces. I couldn't tell him this would not be so.

"I wanted to follow my brother Duane," he said, "but the army caught me so I didn't go 'till I was seventeen."

His voice was thin, watery. I leaned forward to hear him better. "All the boys wanted in back then," he said. "You could almost get in the military without a birth certificate.

"The marines said they had a secure beachhead on that Okanawee, but when the Seventeenth Infantry come in they just slaughtered us. The Japs had overrun the marines." Dorsey rocked a little, and his knuckles gripped the edge of his seat. "Mom got a telegram that Duane was missing in action."

Duane was missing for days by way of a notch in the earth, Dorsey told me. Later Duane would not speak of it, the hours in a muddied frontier, of hearing echoes. In the pressing dark of his trench, it was as if he held up a ceiling with both hands to save what was still inside. Near collapse, Duane may have repeated the word "whiskey" a time or two, for the drink, or in an attempt at radio code the military used when things were unclear—*Alpha-Bravo-Charlie*. Duane might have muttered "Whiskey" for the letter *W*, for such clarity as could be had, and maybe for hope: *Whiskey-Hotel-Yankee*.

After he told me Duane ate K rations out of the pockets of the dead soldiers in the trench, I looked through the car windshield, dazed. Trying to make sense of it, I imagined Duane, his torn military coat, his trembling fingers. Pushing aside fabric, avoiding the touch of cold skin, finding tins of food. Duane eating last suppers for them all, alone in a silent laceration of earth.

"He'd see feet go by and lay there. He played dead for ten days. Finally, he couldn't take no more, and he saw what he thought were American boots. Duane wasn't sure if they'd been stolen off a dead soldier, if he'd get shot or not, but by that time he didn't care. He stuck a hand out and grabbed an ankle."

Dorsey shifted around. "He got sent home."

I pulled the car up to his farmhouse. Dorsey started to inch forward on the seat, moving so his weight was more centered over his feet. His orthopedic shoes were wide and ugly with a Velcro flap over their tops, and they helped him balance. The car window made the back of his head bright from the angle of the sunlight. Wisps of dark hair glistened and waved in the air above his thick glasses. He paused.

"After I got back to Nebraska, me and Duane would go down to North Omaha. It was pretty rough there, but I think he just didn't care much one way or another."

"He didn't fit at home anymore," I said, because I knew.

"He wasn't right," Dorsey said.

He didn't visit the movie hall or other places where you saw the returning men, but found new people in other parts of town. Faces wore shadows there, playing off dark hair, darker thoughts, and teeth that flashed white at the sound of dice hitting a wall.

"Nobody would fight with Duane, 'cause he was the toughest one on the street. Man, could he fight. I couldn't fight like he could; I always got hit too many times. Guys like Duane seemed like they never got hit."

Dorsey sounded so awed at that moment it was as if he had bumped right to the moment of watching his big brother fight and win against any comer.

"One night, Duane said, 'Let's play some dice.' I wanted to know where we were going, but he wouldn't say. We went through the dark alleys, down underneath an old house. We crawled in like a couple of dogs.

"Them days you usually just shot craps against the side of a wall, but there they all were—laying their money out. I says, 'Duane, they're going to kill you if you win,' but he just said, 'Nah, they're my buddies.' I wanted to leave, but I was afraid to go out by myself. So there we all were, playing dice down in that hole, and everyone was just as happy as hell shooting craps."

Dorsey got out of the car and shambled toward his front door as wind blew dust into our lowered faces. I shook my head: my America had been sliced from a different pie. My dad was an engineer, a Shriner, and an Indian. He didn't ride tricycles in the town parades, but he helped with Shriner burn hospital fund-raising, and he and Mom, immigrants from Bengal the year Kennedy was assassinated, had cocktail parties for their Indian friends gathered from across three states—as far as Tulsa to the south, Joplin to the east, and Kansas City to the north—with an ongoing dispute about whether Scotch (Baba) or bourbon (Mom) was best. They served it to friends—well, mostly to the men—at a bar covered in black leather in our family room. "I'll take a Chivas on the rocks," the men said, jingling change in their pockets. There was no sneering. Ice clinked, and people stood chatting on orange-and-brown shag carpet. I was offered sips and always made faces. The women in silk saris sipped their Sprite approvingly.

It was a far cry from Duane's whiskey and dice days, yet we were now family. Earth-contact farmhouses, cows, chickpea flour, and India—we shared the Midwest in different ways.

As we walked to the house from the car, I called out when I saw large rocks, cracks, and clumps of dirt that might have tripped Dorsey up. The screen door slammed behind us as we entered the cool, dark living room.

Dorsey asked for the needle so he could shoot. I read the cc level for him. He pulled up his shirt, pinched a fold of skin, and stuck the needle into his stomach without wincing. He had been doing this for nineteen years, since he was fifty-two.

I glanced at him when he was done and noticed he was looking at his hands. He was nauseated from the car ride, and it had always helped to look out over a wide horizon. But now the view was blurry for him, and that made his nausea worse.

"Duane come out of that basement hole one night," Dorsey said, sitting up. "The one where we played the craps. This was right before he died, and I think it had something to do with it." Dorsey began rubbing his jaw.

"There was about five or six little, ohhh, I'm trying to think what they were, they mighta been Cuban, but there was five or six of them, beating up this boy with a chain on the end of a stick. And Duane said, 'Well, you sons of bitches' and went after them.

"He grabbed one and hit him. One crawled underneath the car and tried to get away, but Duane drug him up and smacked him. There was five or six of those devils jumping on him and kicking at him and hitting him with that chain, and they finally hit him across the head and split his head wide open. Him and that boy went to the hospital that night. They got sewed up. Duane's head swelled up. His eyes, too.

"That was the first time he got beat up, but they did a good job with that stick and chain. They were small people—what the hell were they? Duane told me, but I forget now."

"Why would Duane keep going back?" Even years after the fact, this pull of darkness frightened me.

"Duane was right there among them. They liked him and he liked them."

Dorsey found him alone a month later.

"Duane had headaches so bad from the beating that there were blisters on the insides of his legs as big as saucers from rubbing his knees together. He'd grind them together, I guess. I took him to the hospital, and they got him feeling better. Got rid of the pneumonia they said he had. I'll never forget, I came back to visit and he was all dressed, ready to go, and asked that I get him out of that hellhole of a hospital. He didn't like it. I said I'd get him the next day. The next morning they gave him a pill, and he threw his head back, had a stroke, and died. Thirty-eight years old."

Dorsey went quiet. He looked out the window but didn't really focus.

"There has to be faces to each soul. That church of Ruth's, they don't tell the truth," he said.

IV.

Everyone had loved my brown-sugar apple pie, so the fall after Grandma Cecelia's funeral I brought it again for our Missouri family Thanksgiving. I was careful to make the crust from scratch. I put the pie in a basket and carried it gingerly into Susie's farmhouse not far from Dorsey's place. I was primed. But by the end, there was just one slice carved out of the pie plate. Susie's deep-dish, on the other hand, was all gone.

The next holiday, the phone conversation went something like, "Susie will bring the apple. What are you bringing?"

The brown-sugar apple pie had lost.

"What?" I mumbled in low-voiced distress. "Rum cake," I said.

It was the first thing I could think of. I made rum cake for a local fund-raiser, just an embellished cake-mix cake, nothing fancy, and nothing really special, I thought. But considering Dorsey's sweet tooth and his old stories about whiskey, I thought of a close second, rum. Rum, wrapped in the lore of Barbados and Britain and slave trading and leftover molasses, cheaper than brandy, stronger than beer, was the drink that built colonial America, as cheap molasses made into rum in New England was used to buy slaves for Maryland and the Carolinas, and to pay off English merchants. In the late-seventeenth century, paychecks were in rum, for goodness' sake. Rum was as American as any drink— maybe even more so than bourbon. It could be used to drench a box of cake mix. It was a worthy peer of brown-sugar apple pie. Yes, by golly, I'd do it. I'd drench yellow cake in rum and be redeemed, fit in, blend.

That holiday I eyed the counter of desserts. The rummy essence of my cake eased into the room from among the cheesecakes and Susie's deep-dish pies and fudge. Utensils clanked across the table. The top of the cake looked white from the cream I had beaten earlier. The loosening peaks slid comfortably along the ridge, pooling a little on the sides and leaving hills of creamy invitation. The cake stood quiet and, if I may say so, proud.

"That's my favorite," Ron, my brother-in-law, said.

My shoulders relaxed; my cake was accepted. I looked over with a smile.

"It's the best apple pie ever," Ron said.

I deflated.

The whipped cream slid a little farther down the sides of the cake, collapsing. I turned away. "Nothing to see here," I wanted to say. "Nothing to see."

As the afternoon went by, my rum cake continued to fume on the counter.

I looked at the white mounds of cream, like white elephants against the deeper-colored kitchen tiles. Dorsey began another story, and I half listened in.

"One Saturday morning, Chenk Reiner come to town. He always liked us boys, so he come and asked us if we wanted to help haul hay. That morning, me, Bull Neilson, Bore Tackner, and Two-Gun Smith went out with Chenk and his old tractor."

I smiled at the names of the men, at the enthusiasm in Dorsey's voice, and looked outside. Large cumulus clouds were moving slowly over the land. I felt a shift, barely perceptible. I had let difference define me my entire life, yet I kept myself invisible, clinging to borders quietly. As counterintuitive as it seemed, blending into this family meant letting others see who I was: an Indian woman from Kansas who married a Missouri farm boy and whose culinary vocabulary included both pie pastry and baeshun flour. My own life, I was just beginning to know, was one of the many acceptable ways to be in the world, something I had accorded to everyone but myself.

Dorsey's voice pulled me back to the conversation. ". . . and Two-Gun, he says he can lasso anything, and here comes a '41 Dodge down the road. Those old door handles them days went forward, and you had to pull on them to open the door. Two-Gun was going to lasso the aerial, but he missed and caught the door handle. The car was going that way, Chenk was going this way with the tractor, and the rope was tied to the back of the hayrack. It pulled the door handle right off the guy's car, dumped our hayrack right over."

I had to smile, thinking of hay falling off the truck bed in great tufts and the boys leaping, all of them pulled in two directions. As Dorsey continued talking, I gazed outside and slipped away from the rational world of the kitchen, pulling back, trying to sort my thoughts through.

The land across the farm fields swelled minutely upward. In the middle there was no shade and no trees, and the farmhouse was between two lines of fences in the sun. Close against the side of the house there was the warm shadow of the building and a sliding glass door made of tinted glass and a mesh screen to keep out flies. The farmers and the Indian girl with them sat at a table inside. It was very hot. The family would begin to pack up to go home in forty minutes or so.

"What dessert should we eat?" a young girl asked. She had shaken out her ponytail and laid her hand on the table.

"It's pretty hot," a man's voice said.

"Let's drink tea."

The girl was looking off at the line of the fields. The gentle swell formed a white ridge in the sun. The country was brown and dry. She switched her gaze to the counter.

"It looks like white rum cake," she said.

"I've never tasted that," the man's voice said.

A thick slice was cut into the mass. A forkful lifted. Then another, faster, as the taste filtered over their tongues. A comradery of rum was formed. Another fork lifted; aroma swelled. More slices came away from the plate.

This much I know, seventeen years later, looking back at that moment in the kitchen: Becoming faceless isn't a loss. It is a release into what has always been. That day, I began to see it. At the end of the evening, my cake plate was empty, like all the other women's. We walked to our cars with a suite of containers between us, delighted by the boxed-up slices nabbed from each other for later, reveling in the surprise of family, how we spelled each other with sugar, how we all held up our end.

DAY COME WHITE, NIGHT COME BLACK

DEBRA MAGPIE EARLING

ONE GRAY SEPTEMBER MANY years ago, my grandmother became obsessed with one particular story about a witch with skin the color of sour apples, an ill-tempered hag with dreadfully long fingers made of gnarly twigs. Black pointed hat. Wart on the nose. You know—that witch.

I was thirteen at the time. Titanically bored. Not easily amused or frightened. Besides, who was afraid of that witch?

But when night shadowed the garden and a damp, spicy scent invaded our house, my grandmother told that witch story over and over again, adding a few lines here, a few lines there, until she had fine-tuned her hideous chant—the witch is standing by the bedposts in the old graveyard after dusk . . . see her face in the dusky puddles where the little children splash . . . the witch the witch THE WITCH!!!

My parents urged her to stop, or at the very least tell another story, but Grandmother had become so mean, so spiteful in her dotage, that she began to recite the story at every avail—in the root cellar . . . at the garden's edge . . . at the dining table . . . beside the weeping willow swing . . . even outside the bathroom door. Her endless telling became a colossal bore—an ear-sick trifle to be endured. But as the days passed we began to feel a change, a subtle electric buzzing in the air gaining strength. We couldn't pass one another without hearing snaps of static.

Over the course of that blustery fall, my grandmother fell ill. Her skin cracked open as if struck by the hand of God. A mildew-heavy smell hissed from fissures in her neck. Her body literally outgassed. She fumed greenish clouds. But still, she told the same infuriating story!

The story wheedled into our brains. My father woke screaming every night. My mother—the old Catholic—sought another approach. Every room in our house quivered with votive candles.

No one visited us for pie. No one stopped by for whiskey. Our once elegant house became sadder than a funeral home. To get away from my grandmother and her incessant recitation—the witch is seething in the trees . . . the witch is at the door . . . coming closer . . . coming closer . . . and closer . . . the . . . the witch . . . is . . . at . . . the . . . DOOR!—I moved to the attic. I was thirteen and old enough to be left alone.

Then one night—one dark and terrible night—I woke alone in the attic to a curious sound. A faint cheery noise in the darkness. I convinced myself it was the wind. Nothing more. Certainly nothing to be afraid of. But when I heard the sound again, it seemed to be moving. A pleasant sound like wind through bottle chimes. I became aware that a column of iridescent flies twirled just above my head. The bedsprings sagged and the blankets pulled tight at my feet as if someone, or something, heavy had just plopped down at the end of my bed.

I was paralyzed. The dim, glittery light from the high attic window grazed the witch, and she cast a grim glow in the darkness.

When she grinned, fireflies sparked the air that I soon discovered
were not fireflies at all, but horseflies, the devil's flies, hell-lit
and biting.

I hadn't listened to my grandmother's warning not to sleep on
my belly.

I felt the searing cold of her as the witch climbed on my back.
Her razor-sharp knees sheared the skin from my ribs. Frost lit
the nightstand and curled up in wisps at the windows. A quaking,
shivering freeze lit my heart. I heard bones snap as I hit the floor. My
bones! The witch yanked my long hair as she rode me like a broken
mare across the attic floorboards. Splinters scoured my belly.

I came to my senses poised on the window ledge—set to plunge
forever into darkness. She would have ridden me to Hades. "Whiskey
and pie," she whispered in my ear. "Whiskey and pie."

Years later, when I told my father the story, he said, "It's not
whiskey and pie, you fool. It's whiskey and rye."

EMMA'S REVELATION

When Joseph Smith informed his wife that God had told him he was supposed to have a bunch of new wives, Emma was like, "You've got to be fucking kidding me." But it was written out, of course, God addressing Emma directly, saying, *I command mine handmaid, Emma Smith, to abide and cleave unto my servant Joseph and to none else. But if she will not abide this commandment, she shall be destroyed.* This was what Emma was so tired of. She was supposed to cleave only unto Joseph, while Joseph could cleave unto whomever he wanted, God saying that *if any man espouse a virgin, and desire to espouse another, and the first give her consent, and if he espouse the second, and they are virgins, and have vowed to no other man, then he is justified.* "Joseph," Emma said, "you espouse every virgin," and Joseph was like, "What am I supposed to do? It's God's will." That night an angel of the Lord came to Emma and said, "God didn't really tell Joseph any of that stuff. Joseph just wants to have sex with lots of different women." Emma was like, "But he said it wasn't about the sex," and the angel was like, "They always say that," and Emma was like, "So is all the other crazy shit made up, too?" And the angel was like, "I'm not going to get into that. But here's the revelation. From now on, according to God, Joseph Smith has to do whatever you tell him to do. Wash the dishes. Cook. Anything. All of it. We know how out of control he's been. It's pretty common with prophets, actually. Also, all that bullshit about matrimonial alliances with the natives, Mormon men taking native wives, *that their posterity may become white and delightsome.* That's just insane."

MAKES 2 COCKTAILS

1 sister-wife chore wheel	Bitters	His grandmother's china
Whiskey	2 cherries	
Sweet vermouth	1 Colt Navy revolver	

1 Place the chore wheel on the table. Make a Manhattan. Bourbon or
rye. Doesn't matter. People in Wisconsin use brandy. Who cares?
Sit at the table. Spin the chore wheel. Spin the revolver's cylinder.
Unload it. Load it. You're not gonna hurt anybody. But you've got to
stop putting up with this shit. Arrange his grandmother's china on
the counter, propped on little stands facing you. Scribble *salad plate*
over one window of the chore wheel, *gravy boat* over another. Yes,
you loved him once. So what. Cry if you want to. Cry until you can't
cry anymore. Make another drink. Spin the wheel. Raise the revolver.
Aim at the appropriate piece of china. Everybody wants this. Even his
grandmother. Even those little girls he's lied to. Especially them. One
more sip to steady your hand. Revelate!

YUM YUM RUM CAKE

This recipe (adapted from *Sassafras: The Ozarks Cookbook*) makes a super-moist treat that blends sugar and rum with cream and sugar. If you'd rather have a more firm or less sweet cake, use half the rum sauce. For the full rum cake experience, pour it all on. The original recipe calls for an eighteen-and-a-half-ounce boxed cake mix, but we tested this with what we could find—a fifteen-and-a-quarter-ounce box—and it was just as good. Nina also suggests serving this cake as finger bites by baking the cake in a greased and floured nine-by-fifteen-inch jelly roll pan. Just pour the rum sauce over the cooling cake, wait until it is absorbed, cut the cake into one-inch squares, and eat it all up—with or without the whipped cream.

MAKES 12 SERVINGS

1 box yellow cake mix
1 (3.4-ounce) package vanilla instant pudding mix
¾ cup light rum, divided
¾ cup water, divided

½ cup vegetable oil
4 eggs
1 cup plus 2 tablespoons sugar, divided

½ cup unsalted butter
1 cup heavy cream, whipped

1 Preheat oven to 350 degrees F. Grease and flour a Bundt pan or a 9-by-13-inch rectangular pan.

2 In a large bowl, combine the cake mix with the pudding mix. With an electric mixer on low, beat in ½ cup of the rum, ½ cup of the water, and the oil. Beat in the eggs on medium speed, one at a time, then continue

beating for 2 more minutes on high speed. Pour the batter into the prepared pan.

3   Bake the cake for 40 to 45 minutes if using a Bundt pan, or 25 to 30 minutes if using a rectangular pan. The cake should feel very firm, and a toothpick poked into the center should come out clean. Remove the pan from the oven, and cool for 20 minutes. If using a Bundt pan, keep the cake in the pan.

4   While the cake is cooling, make the rum sauce. In a medium saucepan over medium heat, bring 1 cup of the sugar, the butter, the remaining ¼ cup rum, and the remaining ¼ cup water to a boil, stirring often. Once the sauce boils, remove it from heat and pour it over the cooled cake. Let it sit until fully soaked in, about 40 minutes. Then, if using a bundt pan, remove the cake from the pan.

5   To make the whipped cream, chill a medium metal bowl and electric beaters for at least 15 minutes. Beat the cream on high in the chilled bowl until it forms soft peaks, then slowly add the remaining 2 tablespoons sugar, beating on high as you go until the cream is thick and forms stiff peaks.

6   Garnish the rum cake with whipped cream. Serve immediately. Cover and store leftovers in the refrigerator for up to 3 days.

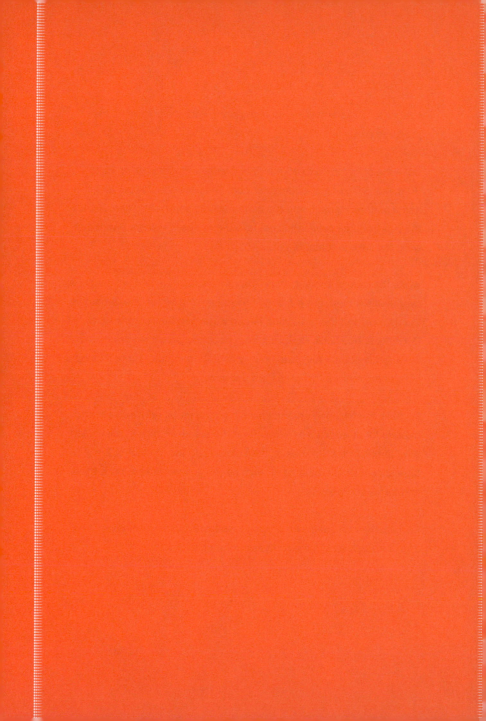

Whiskey is by far the most popular of all remedies that won't cure a cold.

—JERRY VALE

HOH RIVER TRAIL INCIDENT

THOM CARAWAY

The trail ended in a slide, the bank of the river
washed out, spring high runoff from the Olympic range
having chewed at the rock and soil and tree roots until
   it all collapsed,
swallowed by the rush and pushed out to sea.

It's true we searched. It's true we found a moose,
a bear, and no trail. It's true we heard cat sounds,
and camped on a sandbar in the middle of the August river.
It's true cats don't like water.

It's true most of our backcountry trips
were similarly fated. And that we'd planned ahead
this time, not enough to have brought a GPS,
but enough to have brought a bottle of Scotch.

It's true I'd like to like Scotch and it's just as true
that I cannot hold hard liquor. It's true that Jeff
was more than a little both drunk and frightened
at the prospect of becoming a mountain lion's dinner.

It's true that the first rule of the backcountry
is do not entice predators with any strong smells,
as if ninety-eight degrees of meat did not exude enough smell
to attract a big cat from a mile away.

It's true that after finishing the bottle, playing cards,
and smoking many strong-smelling cigarettes,
I threw up directly outside our tent.
It's true that Jeff, still drunk and frightened,

tried to hoist our tent, which still contained most of our gear,
all at once to a new location, though the sandbar
was no more than thirty dry feet. It's true he snapped
one of two poles clean in half, and that I drunkenly

splinted it back together with a tree branch and duct tape,
and that both of us slept through until gray morning
revealed us uneaten and still idiotic.
All of those things are true, and none of them are the story.

In the morning, we packed the gimpy tent, and hoisted ourselves
up the river bank, back in the direction of the trail we'd come in on.
It's true that not only could we not find where the trail continued on,
we could not find, despite following our own inbound tracks, the trail
    back out.

For four hours, in steady rain, we slogged through undergrowth,
incredulous, hungover, and lost. We agreed to head back to the river
where we could follow the bank out, but we couldn't agree
on which way the river was. It's true, I was beginning to worry.

At some point, you'd think, with two poets lost in the woods,
the rain would become a metaphor for something. The inability
to find the trail a grand allusion to our unstarted careers.
But we were just wet and lost.

After splitting the difference to get back
to the river, Jeff, from behind me, said, "Hey,
I recognize that tree." And I will tell you this,
I've never imagined a worse joke, a more

mean-spirited, moronic, passive-aggressive bunch of bullshit
       in my life.
It's true I considered murder then. I had fifty pounds on Jeff,
was carrying trekking poles I easily could have stabbed him with,
and I'd puked. Hell, I could break the empty Scotch bottle
       and brandish that.

Twenty steps later, we were back on the trail, pointed
the right direction. Ten miles up the Hoh River, in the middle
of a temperate rain forest, surrounded by moss-covered fir
and cedar, half-snapped snags, waist-high ferns, and God knows

what animals, and Jeff recognized a tree. In the history
of our long friendship, Jeff and I have hugged each other twice.
One was at my baptism. The other, the first, was the moment
we put our feet back on the trail. This is the story, and it is true.

BLUE VELVET

ELIZABETH J. COLEN

I told him I'd take the dog if he got one, take it *if and when* he died. I had to say *if and when* even though he was eighty-five. I believed saying it could prolong things. Stretch time with possibility. *And/or* I could have said. Or *if* you die. *If* you die I will take it.

*

It was the year the pipeline was going in, coming, burrowing through, strange men wet with summer heat haunting the liquor stores, filling up carts in the Walmart on the weekends.

"It won't go to a shelter, I can promise you that."

"You would drive out here to get it?"

"I would drive out here to get it."

*

I was visiting Kansas from Washington, a twenty-eight-hour drive, sixty-two hours total on the train.

*

It was the year I kissed the girl I'd had a crush on for over a decade, standing in her kitchen in Long Beach, California, while the neighbors fought across the alley, and clocks in her hall (three of them) ticked over past midnight into the morning I would leave. The air coming in from the window tasted salty. Her refrigerator hummed behind us like an angry animal. It made me nervous, and I thought of teeth and some camera watching us.

*

"I'll think about the dog," he said.

I pulled up pictures on the internet of dogs close to him that needed homes.

"I'll think about it," he said.

There was a light across the alley where the fighting continued and the wind blew in, lifting the curtain, and I was pressed between her legs, her ass climbing the counter. I was a decade too late, but decided I loved her.

It had been a week since the kiss, but I hadn't stopped thinking about it. Hours on the train with the landscape dusting by and now tapping on my keyboard scouting mongrels.

*

I would drive back here to get the dog, I said. *If and when.* And I would.

I was visiting in August, as I did every August, taking the train Seattle to Los Angeles (to see the girl), Los Angeles to the middle of Kansas to see him. His Scottish terrier Tyler had just died.

*

The first thing to mention is that Corky isn't my grandpa by blood. If I say *isn't* instead of *wasn't*, will you believe he is still alive?

*

Picasso died within months of his dog, Lump, a seventeen-year-old dachshund. Lump was the only other creature allowed in Picasso's studio. Companion to the artistic process, observer of sketches and strokes.

ELIZABETH J. COLEN

Tyler sat in Grandpa's lap while he watched TV. He sat at Grandpa's feet when Grandpa ate or drank at the kitchen table.

*

Jackson Pollock had a dog, too.

*

"There's something unintentional about drinking in front of the TV. You don't notice what you're doing."

We were sitting at the kitchen table, the bottle of Black Velvet between us. His posture slackened with each round. We were on the fourth.

"Have you ever seen the movie *Blue Velvet*?" I asked him.

"I have not, but I know the song."

I went on to explain the opening scene, the ear in the grass, and regretted it immediately.

"That sounds terrible," he said.

Ice Road Truckers was on in the other room. Loud enough for us to hear it. Something had slid off the road again.

Ours a love I held tightly
Feeling the rapture grow

A show I'd never watched. Grandpa explained the premise, which I could mostly get from the title, the new season's focus, Dalton Road, how to thaw machines in weather like that, how some things never warm up.

Like a flame burning brightly
But when she left, gone was the glow of
Blue velvet

The song was a hit for Bobby Vinton the summer Corky started dating my grandmother. My father was seventeen at the time, and while he was best man at their wedding, they never got along.

Two more glasses of cheap whiskey washed down with a handful of chips and sugar-free hard candies. *Ice Road Truckers* gave over to *Storage Wars* in the other room. Someone was paying too much for a small room full of black garbage bags of children's clothes and VHS tapes. "There's something sinister about that, don't you think," I said, "kids clothes and VHS?" But Grandpa was asleep now, sideways in the hard chair.

ELIZABETH J. COLEN

I tried to wake him and, failing that, sat him more upright, and went to bed.

*

I can still see blue velvet through my tears

*

I hadn't been close to my grandmother. It's a long story about how nobody liked my mom. I saw her and Corky for the first time in seventeen years the summer before she died, when I was passing through–driving Georgia to Washington to start grad school.

*

"I'm glad I saw her," I told him whenever it came up.

"It happened so quickly, as those things do. Tyler was just like that."

*

I was taking the train in another week and a half, going back through Los Angeles, but I wouldn't see the girl.

*

Bluer than velvet was the night

*

The first three nights I was there heat lightning rattled the sky.

Every morning Grandpa made coffee, the TV loud on *American Pickers*, Mike and Frank exploring some old man's barn, the jug of Black Velvet back on the counter next to the bread.

"Toast?" he asked.

"Sure."

Grandpa and I sat at the table, ate toast, and read the morning paper, which like most papers had been reduced to a handful of pages.

Late afternoon, in the heat of the day, I walked across the dry lakebed and back, listening to the dog-day cicadas roar, and watching dust clouds roiling miles in the distance from the pipes going in.

ELIZABETH J. COLEN

I, TOO, SIP FROM THE FLASK

NANCE VAN WINCKEL

The osprey pecks a bit of blue plastic
into her nest of sticks. My brothers, barefoot,
stand in the cold brook
where the dogs are drinking.

Under the wind's icy backside
we woke up in the yard,
our father in the next county
and mother sad in her sister's kitchen—
stringing up dough to dry on steel hooks.

We could drive into town. Someone
would sell us near-beer.
Someone would feed us pancakes.
The boys argue, ankle deep in the muck.

When she shakes them out,
the old bird's wings make the sound of sheets
snapping in a gale. She hates us.
She spits down fish bones.

Last year's version of this year's wind
blew over fake cows in the live nativity.
Striped tails splintered off. Someone had bashed in
the Christ doll's head, and cotton batting—
like a sticky snow—dusted our faces.

My brothers the kings found the doll eyes
in the straw, and have found them twice more
in dreams. We enter the manger's periphery.
A wind without origin tears at us.

We hand over the blue eyes
to the Virgin, who keeps a silver flask
in the folds of her robe. Because,
she says, the cold is so bitter. Kneel now.

THE PEOPLE WHO NEED IT

ROBERT LOPEZ

I don't know what's wrong with the television, but I'm still
a person, still someone that people should know something
about, should maybe feel sorry for, too. What I'm saying is I
turn the television on but can't get a picture. It's the same
thing with the telephone. I pick it up but can't get a dial tone.
Sometimes I think I'm dead, that this is what happens when
you die.

I can look out the window, but this means nothing. I can see
people out there in the world, but maybe they are all dead, too.

The dead people outside are all horrible because they are
dead and dressed in layers because it is cold. Tonight, they
say, it'll be in the single digits.

I remember I was alive once, because I went outside into the
freezing cold and walked to the store and bought pie and

groceries and then brought those pies and groceries home and stored them in the pantry and refrigerator.

I had a job once, too.

How you know you're alive is it's freezing cold and you feel it and it's horrible. How you know you are dead is it's freezing cold and you still feel it and it's even more horrible.

I never prepared a meal for myself, but I always made sure I had plenty of groceries. I never wanted to go to the pantry or open the refrigerator to find it empty.

In the pantry there was flour and sugar and salt, and in the refrigerator there was butter and vegetable shortening. I'm not sure if the vegetable shortening belonged in the refrigerator, but that's where I kept it.

This is what you need to make a pie crust, all you need. Maybe there's more to it, but I don't think there is. I've never made one myself.

No one else has made a pie for me, either, because everyone I know is horrible and doesn't care if I live or die.

I would read pie recipes and collect books about pie and stack them against the wall opposite the window. I wanted books from floor to ceiling.

I had other books, too, but vowed not to read them until I was finished with all the pie books, cover to cover.

I would imagine someone discovering my rotting corpse beneath a pile of books, with pie crumbs still in my beard.

I would buy pies that came in boxes already made, already assembled and baked.

I would stack the pies alphabetically in the pantry, and I would eat pie every night for dinner. Blueberry, strawberry, pumpkin, or plum.

I can't remember the last time I opened the refrigerator or pantry, so I don't know if anything is still in there.

It is colder outside than it is in the refrigerator, the last time I checked. But I can't remember the last time I was outside or the last time I opened the refrigerator.

I also can't remember what my job entailed, what I was responsible for, or how much money I made. I think I did very well. I think I held a prestigious position and had a great many underlings. I remember telling people what to do, and they did it without question, without fail.

The television screen is blank, but I know that it's on. I can hear it buzzing, can hear the inside machinations. There is life inside the television, but there's no proof, no picture.

It might be like my own body. I can hear the heart beating and the blood flowing, the liver groaning and the gall bladder flailing.

It might be too cold for the television to work. It is almost as cold in my apartment as it is outside.

I, too, am dressed in layers, though no one can see this, not even me.

But like the television, I don't have a picture. There are no pictures of me in this apartment, framed or otherwise. There are no mirrors.

There's no sound coming from the television, either, except for that one time. I heard someone who sounded like a game show host talking to people who sounded like contestants.

It's possible that was the job I can't remember: game show host. I have a vague memory of lights and cameras and horrible people acting like imbeciles.

There is the red light indicating the television is on, but it isn't on, not by any measure.

I think the window has been painted shut. I don't know what this means, but I've heard the expression.

I'm not sure how a window can get painted shut, how the paint would keep it shut, why paint would keep it from opening. I don't know if it's a special paint they sell.

I can see my breath, in my home, in the middle of the day.

That I can see my breath doesn't mean I'm alive, I don't think.

People would ask me why I ate pie every night, and my answer was always the same.

Now no one asks me anything. I remember once I had a particular underling even more horrible than the rest, and she would ask me all kinds of questions. She would wear see-through blouses and tight-fitting skirts and open-toed shoes.

I used to call her Ursula the Horrible, though her name was Magdalene.

She would ask me how I got to be on television, how I got my start, what it was like being famous, and if there was anything she could do for me.

I would sit in my chair in front of a giant mirror while they put makeup on me. I'd drink from a coffee cup filled with bourbon and spout curses at random underlings.

One was in charge of keeping my coffee cup filled with bourbon. I'd send this one to the store with a list of which bourbons were acceptable and which weren't.

This one, who was horrible, I think was in love with Ursula. I'd watch him watch her from across a room, a particular look on his face, a mixture of lust and annihilation.

I'd tell him what Ursula did to me last night. I'd make him listen to every single word. I'd ask him what he thought at the end of every single sentence.

I told him we ate pie for dinner, and I said, what do you think of that?

I told him we sat on either side of the table in my kitchen, the pie resting on a hi-hat in the middle of the table, candles flickering between us.

I said, how do you like that?

I told him we didn't even move to the bedroom after we were done, that we took turns on each other right at the table, that she used the pie filling as a massage oil on me, that he wouldn't believe what she did with this filling, how she used it, and how I poured the wax on her one drip at a time until the candle was down to a stump.

I said, how does that work on you?

Before he could answer I walked out of the dressing room.

Actually I don't think this is right, not most of it anyway. I don't think I worked as a game show host with underlings applying makeup and bourbon. I think it was a saloon, one that had swinging doors, like in the old days, like in the movies.

I have a vague memory of dim lights and sawdust and people behaving like imbeciles.

I think this is what Ursula was, an actress. She would wear see-through tops and tight-fitting skirts and open-toed shoes.

I do know the telephone has never rung in my home, and I have never answered it.

The telephone might be ornamental.

This memory of listening to a dial tone for two hours might be a dream or something that I saw on the television back when it was still working.

It's possible I've had both jobs at different times, or it's possible I saw a movie once with a guy who looked like me who had both jobs at different times.

The problem is I can't remember how I used to look, back when I was alive. I think I was very handsome, because I remember Ursula telling me this over and over.

Maybe she thought this would help with her film career. Maybe she was under the impression I had contacts in the business.

The dressing room might've been the back office, and it was always cold back there, like it is here. There was a dartboard and neon signs and a wall calendar with a half-naked girl looking down on everyone.

Ursula would let me take pictures of her when she was half-naked, three-quarters naked, but never fully naked.

I would stand behind the bar and pour drinks for the regulars. I would watch Ursula serving the customers because she was the cocktail waitress trying to be an actress trying to be a movie star. I didn't know how to make most of the drinks, so I would make a whiskey sour or a gin and tonic and I would tell them to drink it.

Tonight, they say, it'll be in the single digits, which is even colder than usual. When I say *they*, I mean the people on the radio. I do have a radio that works, an old transistor.

They say people should beware. They say people should stay home, dress in layers. They are talking about me, I think, but they don't know that I'm already home, already dressed in layers.

Sometimes I think of myself as a contestant on a game show, but I don't know the rules or what I'm supposed to do or if anyone is watching.

I'm not sure if I'm dead, because I've been here for as long as I can remember, and I'm not sure if I miss Ursula or wonder where she is or if she is one of the dead people outside freezing.

The people outside are dead, though they do look alive in most respects.

I see the people every day, but I don't recognize them from one day to the next. I do recognize that almost all of them are dressed in layers and that none of them are Ursula.

Time goes by or it doesn't. I don't have any watches or clocks, and on the radio they never tell me the time, only the weather.

This is what I do to pass the time, if there is time to pass. I look out the window and listen to the radio. I also read from the stacks of books. I am always careful when I remove a book so the others will not fall down all over me.

There is no door here, only the window that's painted shut, but I'm so high up I can't climb out of it into the world below, even if I could open the window, even if it weren't painted shut.

I could probably jump out the window, or maybe not out the window but through it. I'd have to break through the glass to jump out the window.

Sometimes I think about doing this. I'd want to test it first, which is why I think about throwing one of the pie books through the window to see if it'd work.

I probably wouldn't survive the fall. I would be dead once I hit the pavement, if I'm not dead already.

There is also a book in here that I read every day. I start at the beginning and read through till the end.

Each time it is like I'm reading it anew, as I can never remember what the story is about.

It's almost like every day the book tells me a different story.

Today in the book someone fell asleep more or less sitting up after watching birds and squirrels feed from a feeder. There were three different kinds of birds fluttering about and acrobatic squirrels pilfering the bird food whenever they could.

No one mentioned how cold it was, but that's what I assumed, that it was freezing cold. There was no mention of what anyone was wearing, but I imagined all the characters wrapped in coats and scarves.

There was no mention of what the character did for a living, if he was a game show host or a saloon manager or what.

Then this character, the one who fell asleep, his niece, named Chloe, who is almost two in the story, comes into the room, places her elbows on the ottoman where this person is resting his legs, puts her hands together, and clasps them, fingers interlacing with other fingers. She baby talks some gibberish and then leaves.

The character asked his sister if Chloe prays for people, and the sister said, only for people who need it.

I don't know if this is what Chloe does every time in the book, for every reading. Tomorrow she might be a game-show host or an actress. The next day she could be one of those out walking dead in the freezing cold or making pies for people to bring home or mixing drinks in a saloon.

Sometimes I think I wrote this book because I think I once had a sister who had a daughter named Chloe and she was once two years old like the character in the book.

But I can't remember what any of these people looked like or if they looked like anything at all.

I can't remember if this sister or niece ever met Ursula or if they thought she was horrible like everyone else does.

I know Chloe is different from Ursula, because Chloe didn't dress that way or talk that way or eat pie like that. And because it's possible she isn't real, too.

Even still I wish Ursula the best, and I'm glad we don't know each other anymore and that she doesn't know that my television doesn't work and neither does my telephone and I can't remember the last time I tasted pie or bourbon and that I'm freezing to death all alone in here.

What I'm saying is *this* is for Ursula and Chloe, my niece in the story and maybe in real life, too, and by *this* I mean an imaginary bourbon, because I have long since run out, which I raise in salute to these two only, if they are still out there somewhere, certainly freezing, fingers interlaced and clasped, alive or dead, famous or not, working in a saloon or on a movie set, praying for anyone who might need it.

CONGRATULATIONS!
YOU HAVE A NEW MATCH

ELISSA WASHUTA

1. Them:

WHISKEY AND IPAS. Snowboarding is my life. Not looking for anything too serious. Been single for a while now due to avoidance of drama, but I'm ready to put myself back out there for the right girl.

Living my purpose. Just trying this thing out and am down to get a drink so hit me up. Nice guy, not a serial killer, lol. I have near perfect straight teeth for never having braces, and have no clue why I don't smile with my teeth.

Bourbon and Scotch. The kid is my niece. Just moved back to the Northwest. Taking applications for a travel companion. Enjoy a healthy and active lifestyle. Looking for my partner in crime.

Craft beer enthusiast. Not here for hookups. Your average nerd. Podcasts, adventures, movies, guitars, hiking, whiskey, dogs, *Star Wars*, sushi, snack plates, coffee, wine, motorcycles, dancing, drinks, travel, positive vibes, minimalism, bacon, passion. Looking for a discreet lover. Must be fit and in shape.

Beer, whiskey, salsa dancing. School of Hard Knocks, University of Life. 6′1″. Poly dude with a big heart. New to Seattle. I want to beat you at pool. Caring, compassionate, levelheaded, drama free, honest, loyal, humble, passionate, easygoing, funny, adventure seeking, and so on. Looking for a wife to start a family colony.

Entrepreneur. Whiskey, steak, beer, burritos, wine, breakfast, orange juice, cured meats, milk, cheese, coffee, pizza. I am looking for folks to dance with. I want us to be like an old Nintendo console: blow on it hard, and shove it back in the slot.

420 friendly. I love the outdoors. I am that serial killer you have been looking for lol jk. I enjoy meeting people and going out and trying new things. I like to be active but also enjoy staying in. "Follow your passion, be prepared to work hard and sacrifice, and above all, don't let anyone limit your dreams." Must love dogs, be low maintenance, and love hiking.

Living every day like it's my last. I like beautiful smiles. I'm a good guy. Good job. Not an asshole. I love exotic women, and different cultures. What's your fantasy?

Growing old, but never up. Dream big. Work hard. Die living.

2. Me:

When I was fourteen, riding the bus home from school, a boy asked me if he could cut open my chest, pry apart my rib cage with his hands, and rip out my heart.

He was my crush. His name was Salvador D'Angelo, and he was one of a long line of the boys and men I called upon to save me.

"Sure," I said, so I would please him.

He said he was going to wait to open my rib cage. He said it's much easier to pry apart a rib cage than you'd think. In my head, I started calling him *the incubus.* At night, I kept my bedroom window open and hoped he wouldn't come in with the spring air, boy turned demon, broad shoulders as vessels for the unfurling of wings.

I stood at the door to the woodshop classroom and watched his hands. If he had opened my chest, he would have found the hole, bigger than a heart, and a stomach. I thought it was an organ, maybe the *soul* I learned about in Catholic school and imagined as a limp gray sac. The hole had always been there, and when I was little, I filled it with Cadbury Creme Eggs. In high school, I used it as a hiding place for the NyQuil I drank from the Gatorade bottle in my locker. Later, I would keep all sorts of things in the hole: whiskey, Vicodin, cheese, a butterfly knife, Nintendo games, teeth, boxed wine, antipsychotics, condoms. Salvador was expelled for knocking over a soda machine and threatening to kill us all. When he left, nothing changed, like always.

3. Us:

I've selected a stranger again. He sits down. I sit down. He looks just like his pictures. I know he can see the hole. I try to fill it with whatever he wants to see. I can see his teeth when he speaks. He drinks whiskey. I drink soda. I look at his hands and imagine them inside my chest. I swear he's looking at me like he's going to be the one who saves me.

WHITEY ON THE MOON

Am I the only person here who hates space? I mean, it's nice at night and everything—stars, moons, planets, whatever. The northern lights. The southern lights. The western lights. Black holes. Wormholes. Spider holes. Heaven up there in the heavens. But who would want to go *into* space is what I want to know, when there's no oxygen up there to breathe? When your space suit's filled with urine? People went to the moon years ago to play golf and drive dune buggies around. Monkeys and dogs were sent earlier, a fetal pig maybe. David Bowie and Elton John staged a song competition to see who could be sadder about being in space. Bowie won. Meanwhile lots of money was spent going to the moon. A powdered breakfast drink was invented. It was the space age, and it was fantastic.

MAKES 2 COCKTAILS

A recording of Gil Scott-
  Heron's "Whitey on the
  Moon"
72-ounce container Tang
  orange drink mix

Cold water
Hot water
At least 2 toilets
At least 2 lamps
Whiskey

Sweet vermouth
Bitters
2 cherries

1 Put the music on loop. You're going to be listening to it all night. Dump
   2 scoops of Tang into a champagne flute. Add cold water. Smell the
   beverage you've made. Now pour it down the drain. Make another
   one—2 scoops Tang, 1 cup cold water. Pour it down the drain. Are you
   listening to the Gil Scott-Heron? Good. Then you know this line: "No hot
   water, no toilets, no lights / But Whitey's on the moon."

Gather the hot water, the toilets, the lights. Drive them away and don't come back until you're rid of them. Keep listening to Gil Scott-Heron. "A rat done bit my sister Nell / With Whitey on the moon." Once your errands are over, come home and make a Manhattan. I use bourbon, but you can also use rye. People in Wisconsin use brandy. No one knows why. Some people insist a Manhattan must be served up. Do you believe these people? They should be beaten, soaked in Tang, shot into space. Sip your drink. Are you still listening to the music? Good. Tap the rhythm on the table. Say the words along with Gil Scott-Heron. "A rat done bit my sister Nell . . ." Sip your drink. If you think of yourself as a taxpayer first, a citizen second, try to figure out what's wrong with you. Maybe it's not too late.

POSSIBLY BLUEBERRY PIE

This recipe could become a raspberry pie or blackberry pie if you substitute those berries for blueberries, or a cherry pie if you sub cherries and add a half teaspoon almond extract, or an apple pie if you double the lemon and lower the flour to three tablespoons, or a banana-cream pie if you replace everything except the bottom crust with bananas and pudding and add some whipped cream, or a pecan pie if you do like banana-cream pie but with pecans and sugar and forget about the whipped cream. What I'm saying is that pie is just one or two crusts and four or five or six cups of filling. Make a blueberry pie or don't. Peach pie's good, too. Maybe you're not hungry.

MAKES ONE 9-INCH PIE

1 recipe Pie School Pastry Crust (see page 241)
5 cups fresh or frozen blueberries
½ cup granulated sugar

Juice of ½ medium lemon (about 1½ tablespoons)
Pinch kosher salt
5 tablespoons flour
2 tablespoons chilled unsalted butter, cut into small chunks

Egg-white wash (1 egg white beaten with 1 teaspoon water)
Demerara sugar, for sprinkling

1   Prepare the dough, and refrigerate it for at least 1 hour or up to 3 days.

2   Roll out the bottom crust on a floured surface and place it in a 9-inch pie plate. Tuck the crust into the plate and trim the edges. Refrigerate the crust while you prepare the next steps of the recipe.

3   Preheat the oven to 425 degrees F.

4   In a large bowl, mix the blueberries, granulated sugar, lemon juice, and salt. Taste and adjust the granulated sugar, lemon, or salt as necessary. Add the flour and butter, and stir to combine. Set aside.

5   Roll out the top crust on a floured surface, and retrieve the pie plate from the refrigerator.

6   Pour the filling into the bottom crust, mound it with your hands, and drape the top crust over it. Trim, fold, and flute the edges. Cut generous steam vents, brush the crust with the egg-white wash, and sprinkle it with Demerara sugar.

7   Bake the pie in the middle of the oven for 10 to 15 minutes, until the crust is blistered and blond. Reduce the heat to 375 degrees F, and bake for 35 to 45 minutes more, until the crust is deeply golden and the juices bubble slowly at the pie's edge. Rotate the pie front to back halfway through to ensure even baking.

8   Cool the pie on a wire rack for at least 1 hour. Serve warm or at room temperature. Store leftovers on the kitchen counter, loosely wrapped in a towel, for up to 3 days.

6

The whiskey on your breath
Could make a small boy dizzy

—THEODORE ROETHKE, "MY PAPA'S WALTZ"

PIE AND WHISKEY

MELISSA KWASNY

My girls prefer their whiskey straight with ice.
Though pie's okay, it doesn't get us loaded,
and high is what we want, these days averse
to logic. I won't mention Trump. He's sordid.

Why not instead discuss the WNBA?
How Brittney Griner at six eight can dunk,
or Shoni Schimmel, off the rez, her plays
behind her back, the funky pass, then sunk

by Angel. If we don't watch them, who?
So Brittney and her wife fought on the floor.
We shout: Oh, Lana Turner, we love you,
get up. You make us all look bad—and bored.

That marriage is not all, we all agree.
Yet love. Love is the answer, Lennon said.

Sweetie pie, it's not a matter of decree.
And look, the NRA would shoot him dead.

I walk the roads in evening smoke, the fires
are indication of our real
dilemma. The planet heating up, the crises.
While controversies rage at AWP.

I did not go to Smith or Reed, nor do
I wear Doc Martens. What are preferences?
Though everybody thinks we're hip and cool
you probably do not get my references.

Elena Delle Donne, who we thought straight,
and handsome Candace Parker with a child—
so what? They both shoot 90, 98
percent at the free-throw line. This scansion's wild,

I know, and out of date. But Skylar Diggins,
Ogwumike—the sisters show no mercy—
(you have to blame these rhymes on Mister Ligon)
Rebekkah Brunson, Bonner, and Dupree,

Seimone Augustus, Epiphanny Prince, Sue Bird,
and Maya Moore. Taurasi! Russians pay
her more than us to sit it out. Absurd!
It's here we see our own are on display.

Especially from me, this poem's strange.
The topic's queer, if not especially risky.
We're 10 percent, we're legal. We're free range.
It's queerer still to combine pie and whiskey.

CROSS THE WOODS

JESS WALTER

OH, THAT FUCKING PETER PAN hit-and-run cocksucker. Thoughtless asshole. Selfish prick. Not that she should be surprised; Marcus was a runner, a bolter. He always left in the dark. "It's like dating Houdini," she used to tell her friends. Maggie could handcuff him, straitjacket him, lock him in a steamer trunk, and at three a.m., the stupid commitment-phobe would tiptoe out in the dark, belt undone, shoes in hand.

"Yeah, I'm not big on *Good morning*," he used to say, shorthand for *I'm going to keep fucking other women.*

So, no, it wasn't that she was surprised. Marcus was a few months younger than she was, an immature, womanizing tool when they'd met three years ago. Which was okay then. After a year of shotgun marriage and six months as a single parent, the last thing Maggie wanted was another lousy husband. But she *had* expected the relationship to grow, Marcus to evolve. But how could someone so happy with himself ever change?

No, honestly, what bothered her ... was that it *bothered* her.

She'd known just what she was getting last night with Marcus. It wasn't like she'd wanted to elope. She'd wanted just this: to feel his weight, to lose herself. *Marcus inside.*

So why did waking up alone now make her feel like such a failure . . . as a feminist or an existentialist . . . or what? Shouldn't it be enough to get laid? To smell him in her bed, to see the indentation in the other pillow, think like a guy, like him: *Good fuck. Right. Move on.*

Instead she felt empty and on the verge of tears, certain she would spend the rest of her life as a pathetic, bitter single mother, as a bullshit cliché—her thoughts looping into a women's magazine quiz she'd taken during the whole Marcus breakup ("Will He Ever Commit?") and then, worst of all—to her mother's pet word, *used.* Of all the words—*used*? No one had used anyone, so why did she feel fucked and put away? She had the urge to sue someone, her mom, or Marcus, or those girls from eighth grade, or the Catholic Church, or to organize a class-action suit against the makers of that word, *used.*

Maybe it was just time and place, the circumstances that made her feel so awful, the shock of seeing him last night for the first time in six months, having him show up at the wake like that. ("Your dad would've hated that I was here, huh?") Marcus looked great in a suit—my god, those cyclist's shoulders and hips— and then the Jameson started flowing and the stories, and it was nice to laugh, and Marcus half apologized for not calling for so long ("I had some growing up to do,"), and even if it was bullshit, it was . . . nice, and when they were walking to their cars she practically willed him to say something, anything, so when he looked over in the parking lot and said, simply, "Well . . ." that was all it took; she was helpless, incapable of coming up with a pro-con list . . . or a thought, because at that moment there were only two things in the universe: alone and Marcus. And last night she could not do alone.

Maggie sat up in bed. She looked down. All sag and slump. Was there any lasting benefit from something like last night, any residue?

Yesterday, it had been six months since she'd had sex, and today it has been six hours. But did being touched have any weight the next day, any value? It wasn't like she could feel his hands anymore, like she could feel anything—except sadness. A yawning sense of *alone*. Whiskey in her throat, in her throbbing head. Maggie opened her nightstand for some Advil, and that's when she noticed, in the corner, on the floor behind the bathroom door, in a heap, a gray suit jacket.

She heard faint voices then, from the kitchen. She got out of bed, pulled her robe on, and went downstairs.

In the kitchen Dustin stood on a chair, facing Marcus. They were eye to eye, each holding neckties. They were a foot apart, shirtless, and they had the ties looped around their bare necks. Marcus was in his boxer briefs, Dustin in his *Transformers* pajama pants.

"Do what I do," Marcus said. "Like looking in a mirror."

Shoulder blades jutted from Dustin's tiny pale back.

"Cross the woods," Marcus said.

"Cross the woods," Dustin said.

"Over the hill," Marcus said.

"Over," Dustin said.

"Around."

"Around."

"Behind."

"Behind."

"And through."

"And through."

"Perfect. Now turn around and show your mom," Marcus said.

Dustin turned. He beamed, surprised to see his mother in the doorway.

"Look," Dustin said, "I'm wearing Grandpa's tie."

The tie was blue, with little red sailing flags. It hung past Dustin's feet. He must've gotten it out of the box in the living room that

Maggie's stepmother had sent home with her. It was looped in the sort of unmanageable knot Dustin always got in his sneakers.

Maggie wondered then if there wasn't just one ache in the world: sad, happy, horny, drunk, sorry, satisfied, grieving, lonely. If we believed these to be different feelings, but they all came from the same sweet unbearable spring.

Marcus had made coffee. He handed her a cup. She put it to her lips until she could speak again. Finally, she said to her son, in a half whisper, "It looks so good on you, baby."

THE CHILDREN'S THEATER

ED SKOOG

One morning I'll leave the house naked
and stroll down the street, fun for everyone
to be relieved from shame for a moment,
nourishment for my inner scold.
Most people I've seen, I've seen clothed.
What anyone wore I don't remember,
while the people I've seen nude
I remember everything about, or can I
draw the first nipple I kissed by video light
or the cyclorama of middle school showers,
all of us in awful proportions, half kid, half dude.
Classmates with the largest dicks
have been first to die, by misadventure,
cancer, problems of the liver. Still,
most Swedes debut sexually at fifteen
and in China it's twenty-three.
Everyone in this floating world is naked.
I'm tired of having a body. The mind's a bore,

too, with its video light. On their patio,
my neighbors talk about their bodies
in low voices while the bug zapper
administers its anonymous questionnaire.
Last week I went for an HIV test
at the free clinic below the repair shop
for musical instruments, also
housing a children's theater,
and I could hear them improvising
as I waited twenty minutes for my blood
to signal the presence or absence
of antibodies. The woman who
administered my test and an anonymous
questionnaire did not believe my story,
though it was both rehearsed and true:
the gas station in Nevada, the basin
where I washed up after hours dazed
on the road bloody with a stranger's
inner life covering my hands,
my face before I noticed. I remember
going to the traveling show of *Sweeney Todd*
in which my cousin Stuart, trained for opera,
submitted his throat to the "demon barber's"
stage knife, sending his body down
the ingenious chute, where Angela Lansbury
baked him into pie. His only sung Sondheim:
"A lavabo and a fancy chair." *Lavabo,*
from the Psalms: "I will wash my hands
in innocency, so will I compass thine altar."
But it just means a sink to wash the blood.
Whose blood. You don't get more naked
than blood. At the clinic, mine dotted

a simple device to rehearse its speech.
I answered her questions of history, sexual
partnerships, gender, gender preference.
Whether rough or high, or had traveled
to any of the following countries.
Behind the wall's frank posters and the plush
toy vulvas piled in the corner, some children's
play dreamed itself into being. We know
without being told that theaters are haunted.
They share with graveyards the whistling taboo,
the seatbacks curved like tombstone tops.
It's the stage manager's job to make sure
a light is left on in that cavern when the last
actor's gone home, stagehands to the bar:
the spirit light, one bulb to keep company.
Of course, my blood maintained its old narrative,
and I left with my burden lifted, or shifted.
Behind the wall, child actors assembled comedy.
Because my cousin had done it, and family
spoke proudly of him, I wanted to be an actor
and made the customary adolescent gestures
toward it. Angela Lansbury and Len Cariou
signed his portion of the AIDS Memorial Quilt
the way we signed one another's playbills
after the run of a high school play, some inside
jokes that even we forget the story of, that mask
the love between people who wear masks.
Not much was said of him after that, alas.
Plays scare, endear me, even a children's summer
production, or wherever in suspended belief
a figure steps forward, outstretches
costumed hand, and pronounces my name.

MARRIAGE (PIE) (II)

J. ROBERT LENNON

HE SAYS, So that's it?

That's it, she says.

It's over, you're saying.

That's what I'm saying, she says.

He stares at her, and she stares back. It's a staring contest. She wins. He looks down at his hands, which are clenched together on the kitchen table.

Now what, he says.

She says, One of us has to move out.

Well, it isn't going to be me, he says.

It's going to have to be, she says, because it isn't going to be me, and that leaves you.

I found this place, he says.

I make more money than you, she says.

He says, But I paid more of the down payment.

With money you owed me, she says. Because I helped you buy the scooter.

We co-owned the scooter!

You're the one who used it, she says.

You're the one who wrecked it!

That's your fault, she says. You didn't tell me it needed new tires.

It didn't!

Anyway, she says, getting up, this place is closer to my office than it is to yours. You'll want a place near your office.

Says who! I like walking from here!

No, you don't, she says. You always complain about the panhandlers and the hipsters and the loud buses.

Those are general complaints about city life, he explains.

Well, she says. Maybe you should move away from the city, then. You could rent a cabin somewhere. Write that novel you always wanted to write.

Novel?

Yeah, she says.

I don't want to write any novel, he says.

Sure you do, she says, walking out of the room. Everybody wants to write the Great American Fucking Novel.

He follows her into the bedroom, where she has lain down and picked up a magazine. He says, So who's going to call June and Theo?

What do you mean?

To tell them we're not coming, he says.

Who said anything about that?

He stares at her. She stares back. It's a staring contest. She wins. He looks at her feet, which are motionless and bare, and says, We're divorcing. We're not going to spend the weekend visiting June and Theo.

Of course we are, she says.

Well, you can, he says. I'm staying here.

No, you're not, she says. Theo is *your* friend. We've been avoiding this visit for months. Now we have to go.

We don't have to do anything!

You're going to need friends after we divorce, she says. Theo's been divorced. You can talk about that. Out on the back patio, drinking whiskey. You can tell him what a horrible bitch I am.

He already knows that, he says.

She says, Touché.

If anything, he says, *you* should stay home. You can't stand June.

That's not true, she says, weakly.

After they left here last time, you said she was the shallowest cunt in Pennsylvania.

She chuckles. Yes, she says, I did.

So why do you want to go?

I'm going to need friends, too, she says, and turns the page of her magazine.

June? You want June to be your friend?

Of course, she says. I don't want friends who are smarter than I am. I want friends I can manipulate.

Well, he says, at least you're being honest.

She says, My honesty is one of my best qualities.

That's true.

And one of yours is your willingness to admit defeat.

That's true.

You'd better pack, she says. And then you can sleep on the couch.

Why do you get the bed? he asks her.

She cracks her toes. I'm already on it, she says. Do you want to try to take it from me?

He tries to think of a witty retort. After a few moments, he admits defeat and goes to the closet to pack.

She drives. In the car, she swears at other motorists inside the city limit, and then she swears at them on the expressway, and then she swears at them on the divided highway that leads to June and Theo's house. Eventually they are on a road too remote to be burdened with traffic, and she swears at the forest.

Look at that fucking shit, she says. It's full of serpents and trolls. And deer, probably.

What's wrong with deer? he says.

Are you going to tell me you like deer now? she shouts. Obviously your head's so full of sentimental Bambi-ass bullshit that you can't see the truth. Which is that deer are the fucking roaches of the forest. They're disease-ridden tick magnets, and their meat tastes like flop sweat. Imagine living out here, surrounded by the things. Human-size rats with fucking coatracks on their heads.

You're in a good mood, he says.

Her face makes something like a smile. I am, she says.

Why? he asks her. Everything is terrible.

I guess I'm contemplating life alone in the house, without you. He says, Oh.

I'm going to strew magazines everywhere, lying open to the articles I'm never going to finish reading. I'm going to spill coffee on things and just leave it there. I shall fart openly, in whatever room I want, and I'll get to do whatever I like, whenever I like, which is basically nothing, all the time.

Sounds great.

It is great, she says. It's my future. As soon as we get through this bullshit weekend with our garbage friends.

You're the one who insisted on coming, he says. I was content to stay home.

You shouldn't call it home anymore, she says. You're moving out.

I haven't agreed to that.

Sure you have.

No, I haven't.

She shrugs. You have in your mind, she says. It's as good as done.

He considers replying, then decides against it. Instead, he presses his forehead to the window and stares out at the deer-infested woods.

June and Theo's house is large and tidy and situated on a cul-de-sac in a quasi-suburban neighborhood near the college where Theo teaches economics. He went to school with Theo. They played Ultimate Frisbee together, an athletic contest for people who like to smoke weed and drink themselves stupid. Neither he nor Theo do much of these things anymore, but Theo likes to pretend that drunken, stoned antics are forever just around the corner. This is annoying, but Theo is the only friend he has who makes any kind of effort with him, and he feels duty bound to respond in kind.

June, a fussy, pretty woman who wears a lot of jewelry, meets them at the door and says, Look at you! Just look at you two!

He glances at his wife, afraid of what she will say. What she says is, Look at *you*!

No, I mean, just *look* at you! June says.

No, look at *you*!

June appears uncomfortable. She turns to lead them into the house, and he elbows her.

Why did you do that? she says, loudly enough for June to hear. Why did you hit me with your elbow?

Sorry, he says.

Theo greets them in the kitchen. He is wearing a big floppy hat. My dermatologist told me it was time! he says. I'm getting to be that age!

She says, To wear hats indoors?

Ha-ha! Theo says. We can always count on you for a laugh! Can't we, June?

We sure can, June says without enthusiasm.

Theo takes a couple of beers out of the fridge and beckons him out to the patio. He follows, glancing at his wife over his shoulder.

She is eyeing June hungrily. A few moments later he and Theo are sitting on a pair of cushioned chairs facing the trees. He thinks, I'm not going to tell Theo we're getting divorced. It's too painful to discuss.

Ha-ha, remember Zoober? Theo says. Remember Kwan? Remember that one time?

Ha-ha, yeah, he replies.

Theo says, Man, where did Lopez get that sweet bud, am I right? I couldn't tell my ass from my ankle.

We're getting divorced, he says.

What! Theo exclaims. You two?

He nods.

I thought you two would be together forever!

Really? he says. We fight constantly and are unpleasant to be around. Our parents agreed that our union would be an expensive mistake.

Sure, but still, says Theo.

How do you and June do it? he asks. You seem so happy.

Oh, I dunno, Theo says, gesturing with his bottle of beer. Stamina. Inertia. We've had a rough patch here and there.

What kind of rough patch?

Oh, Theo says, you know. June's a hypochondriac and shoplifts, and I don't like sex. But we're pretty solid, I think.

Oh. Well, he says. I'm curious. Do you ever hear from your first wife? Are you . . . friends?

First wife?

Yes. You were married before June, right?

No, no, Theo says.

I'm sorry, he replies. I thought you were divorced.

I was, Theo says. I divorced June. Then we got married again.

I see.

We just belonged together! Theo says.

I guess you did.

So, Theo goes on, clearing his throat, what's next for you two? Is she moving out?

He takes a sip of his beer, which turns into a long draft, which turns into the bottle being empty. No, he says, glumly. I am.

In the kitchen, she is listening to June talk. June is making a pie, but this isn't preventing her from talking. June is multitasking, with the two tasks being talking and making a pie. June says, I've been to four doctors, and none of them can figure out what's going on with my neck.

I was going to say, she replies. What's up with her neck?

June says, Really? You noticed?

It's in your carriage, she says. I took one look at you, and I thought, that neck is super wrong.

June is energetically mixing some kind of dough. June says, It's just like what happened with my bowels last year. I can't tell you how many colonoscopies I had. Have you ever had one?

Oh, haven't we all, she says.

So then you know, June says. Sorry I have to do this now, June adds. It's for my bereavement group tomorrow.

So it isn't for us, then? You're making a pie but not for us?

Yeah, no, like I said, June says, turning to a bowl of fruit and setting upon it with a masher. There's ice cream in the freezer, for you. After dinner. Which I think Theo is grilling.

We're getting divorced, she says.

I'm mostly over Kibble's passing, June says, mashing fruit, but the group is still very helpful. And I think I'm helping others by being there. I thought about canceling tomorrow, being as you're here, but Theo said to me, June, no, they need you, your experiences are valuable to the group. So I'm making this pie. I'm sorry, what did you say?

We're getting—

June silences her with a hand. She has suddenly frozen in place, her head at a strange angle. June says, Oh God. See? Oh, holy mother of Jesus. My neck.

The masher clatters into the fruit bowl. June's hands are crabbed and trembling. She speaks through gritted teeth.

Help me out here. Hey. Would you?

She gets up from her seat and moves to the kitchen island, then places her hands on June's shoulders. She massages them gently, then firmly. She moves her fingers up to June's neck and squeezes and probes. June groans and lets out a small, plaintive squeal.

Thank you. Oh, thank you, June says.

No problem, she replies.

After a dinner of some kind of casserole and some kind of salad, and a dessert of frost-furred vanilla ice cream from the freezer, the four of them take a walk along the footpaths through the woods. June and Theo forge ahead carrying polished walking sticks they made themselves, from fallen branches. June is limping and saying something about her knee, and Theo nods as if listening.

She and he lag behind. He says something to her in a low grumble that she can't quite hear.

What? she says. Speak up.

I said, he says, I want the sofa. It's the best sofa I've ever had, and it's mine, and I'm going to take it.

In that case, she says, I get the camera.

It's not *the* camera, he says, it's *my* camera. You don't even use it.

I think I will, she says, from now on.

No, you won't! he says. You'll never take pictures of things, because you don't like things. You hate them!

She says, I think I'll learn to appreciate things by photographing them, with my camera.

Fine, he says. You can keep the sofa.

Oh, good. And the camera? she says.

No, not the camera! he says.

I think I'll keep the sofa and the camera, she says, as though to herself. That's a nice combination.

He stares at her, and, after a moment, she stares back. It's a staring contest. She wins. They walk together in silence for a while, and then he says, Theo tells me that he doesn't like sex and that June shoplifts.

Don't judge, she replies.

You don't get to tell me that! he says. You are literally the most judgmental person I have ever known! Anyway, I'm not judging, I'm just saying. Also, Theo told me that his first marriage was also to June. He divorced her and then married her again.

People never learn, she says.

See! he says. There you go! That's judgment.

She says, By the way, June made you a pie.

Really? he says. That pie is for me?

She told me it was, she says.

He says, What kind of pie is it?

Fruit.

I like fruit, he says.

I think she wants to sleep with you, she says. On account of Theo not liking sex. The pie is a metaphor.

It's also a pie, though, he says.

It's both.

They walk in silence for a while until her face makes something like a smile and she points and says, Look! A deer!

He wakes up in the middle of the night and can't get back to sleep. It's cooler out in the country, among the trees, so Theo and June keep the air-conditioning off and the windows open. The open windows disturb him, and the night sounds of the forest disturb him, and his estranged wife's presence in the bed disturbs him, though her absence from it would probably disturb him more. Oh well, he thinks. He'll have to get used to it.

After a while he gets out of bed and tiptoes down the dark stairs to the kitchen. He opens the refrigerator and takes out a carton of milk. He pours himself a glass and microwaves it until it's warm. Then he takes a seat at the table and sips his warm milk.

It's then that he notices the fruit pie, which has been left on the table to cool in the shadows. It's beautifully made, with a crusty brown lattice supporting lots of little pastry leaves. Up from underneath them the fruity filling has bubbled and settled, leaving syrupy traces that are probably sweet and chewy.

He thinks of what his estranged wife has told him and goes to the cabinets for a plate. He finds a fork and a cake server and uses these items to serve himself a large piece of the fruit pie.

It's delicious. He eats the entire piece, washing it down with warm milk, and when he's finished he gets up and helps himself to more milk and more pie.

Halfway through the second piece, though, he is interrupted by June, who has moved stealthily into the moonlit room. She has a strange bearing; her arms are extended and bent, as though supporting a large tureen filled to the rim with hot soup. She is mumbling to herself and, in her sheer nightgown, looks very attractive.

He realizes that, though her eyes are open, June is asleep. She's sleepwalking. She drifts over to the kitchen island and speaks incoherently while making motions with her hands. She would seem to be pantomiming the acts of cooking and complaining.

Impulsively, he stands up and goes to her. Her takes her by the shoulders and speaks her name. Then he takes her into his arms and begins to kiss her on the mouth. For a few seconds her lips move as if in response to his kisses, but he soon realizes that she has merely continued to talk. He experimentally fondles her breast, and she wakes up and takes an awkward step back.

What are you doing! Where am I! What's happening!

He doesn't know what to say, so he just stands there.

Did you touch me! Did you kiss me! Why are you in my kitchen!

I couldn't sleep, he says. I came down and ate some pie.

What pie!

The fruit pie, he says. It's delicious.

Still blinking away sleep, she glances frantically around the room. Her gaze lands on the half-eaten pie and half glass of milk, and she emits a piercing shriek.

My pie! You ate my pie!

It's very good, he reiterates.

It's for my group! My bereavement group! You ate my pie! You kissed me!

Well, he says.

You grabbed my tits! You ate my pie!

What's going on? demands Theo, who has just entered the room wearing a union suit and an actual peaked nightcap, like a character in a Christmas movie. He flicks a switch, and the room is bathed in light. June? he says. Is everything all right?

June points and says, He ate my pie, violated my personal boundaries, and woke me up while I was sleepwalking!

Did you wake my wife up from sleepwalking? Theo says.

I suppose so, he admits.

Don't you know how dangerous that is? That's my wife! Theo shouts. This is my house!

These statements are superfluous both in the volume with which they are spoken and the information they convey. He says, I know. I'm sorry.

People have been known to suffer cardiac arrest when awoken from sleepwalking! Theo loudly informs them.

Also, June adds, I'm personally violated! And my pie!

I think you need to leave, Theo says, then adds, And to think we were once Ultimate buddies. We went through that thing together that one time! I can't believe it.

I'm sorry, he says again. Then he hears the voice of his estranged wife.

What the fuck is going on here? she demands, coming down the stairs.

Theo and June explain the situation, accurately, if overemphatically. She nods, listening, and then turns to him. She says, How can you be friends with these ridiculous fuckwads?

Theo says, Hey—

I've never met a more irritating, self-deluding couple of backwoods dumbasses in my entire life, she says. Was this garbage the best your stupid college had to offer? You'd've been better off making friends with the fucking Frisbee.

She addresses herself to Theo. You, she says, are a pathetic excuse for a man. You sound like a cockatoo, and you look like a fucking Hummel figurine. Talking with you is like being smothered in your sleep with a pillow. You should cut your dick off and feed it to a dog.

And you, she says, turning to June, are a miserable shit with the IQ of a box turtle and a butt like a paper sack of doughnut holes. You dress like you're in a Laura Ingalls Wilder fetish porno. The most important thing in your life is a dead cat, and your bathroom is dirty.

This man, she shouts now, pointing, is my husband. He is a thousand times the human being either of you will ever be, and you should be dry-humping the ground he walks on. You don't deserve to have your boob grabbed by him, your fucking nature trail walked on by him, or your pie eaten by him. If I ever catch either one of you so much as giving him the stink eye, you will find my Doc Martens ankle deep in your hemorrhoid-encrusted assholes so fast you'll wonder if you just time-traveled back to freshman year at fisting school.

Husband! she commands, pointing to the stairs. Get our bags. We are leaving this shitbox in five minutes.

In the stunned silence that follows, she sits down at the kitchen table, picks up the fork, and begins to eat what is left of the fruit pie.

In the car, she says, It was nice catching up with them.

Thank you, he says. For defending me.

She says, You're welcome. I guess you can keep the sofa.

And the camera?

And the camera.

Well, he says. Thanks for that, too.

Or, she says.

Or?

We could just stay married.

He doesn't say anything for a moment. The dark woods rush by outside.

Is that what you want? he asks her.

What I want, she says, is for the world to not be such a fucking kingdom of shit and for all the assholes to dry up and blow away. I want all pain to be erased from my memory, and I want to spend the next fifty years in a state of effortless euphoria until I die peacefully in my sleep and ascend to a heaven of puffy clouds, cute interspecies animal friendships, and incessant orgasms at the nimble hands of the men's Olympic diving team.

Okay, he says.

Also, that pie, she says. I want to eat more of that dumb bitch's pie.

I think, he says, that your other wishes might be more easily fulfilled.

Her face makes something like a smile. His does, too. He stares at her, and she stares back. It's a staring contest. Then a deer leaps onto the road and is briefly illuminated by their headlights before tumbling over the hood and crashing into the windshield. The airbags deploy, catching their bodies as they lurch forward; their eyeglasses fly off, and the car comes to a swerving, shuddering halt.

The airbags deflate. Her hands reach out for him. Are you all right? she says. Are you all right?

Yes, he says.

She says, It was a fucking deer. I knew it. Did you see that? Are you all right?

I saw it, he says. I'm all right. Are you all right?

I'm fucking pissed, she says.

Her hand finds his hand. They hold hands.

He says, Good.

STORY PROBLEMS

MAYA JEWELL ZELLER

THE SQUARE ROOT OF whiskey is water. The square root of you is
your father. You follow him down the hallway where he turns left
and left again into a wall. He slumps there, half-drunk. He stands,
half-awake. He banks his shot off the rail into the side pocket. It's
cutthroat you're playing, not like the fish, but the billiards game with
the hard balls, the cue stick slightly warped so it wobbles when you
check it. The square root of a cue is warped by water. The square
root of Jesus is water into beer. That's the way the story is told here,
where the square root of beer is your father, himself the square
root of God. He knocks another in, so you're stranded over here
by the corner with your balls nearly touching, like Adam reaching.
Here, the square root of morning is Adam punching God in the face.
In this part of America, Adam punches God in the face. It's almost
morning; the sun sneaks around the darkness and creases in the
blanket your mother has hung to keep out the light. Somewhere
above you the stars blink off, and you know there's work to be done,
a cord of wood to split and stack, your brother's back to bend. The

square root of your mother is waiting for you in the dim of her room, naming ferns for the sister you hope will come out of the woods. The trees there are square, their roots square, their leaves. You've been playing all night while the rain falls and the river gets higher. You may or may not make it home on these roads. If you do, you may or may not find it in flames. But the billiards game: the name of the third player evades you. It may be the devil. It may be the square root of a story, an equation, an imaginary number spiraling off the edge of the page. Home may be the square root of these roads. The roads are full of the dark squares of sky they've been named for. In the field full of water where nothing is named for itself, the days are only hours long. You reach for your mother, who holds out a fern. It's a maidenhair. You're that close. You're drunk on the possibility of going somewhere. The square root of the river breaches the square root of its banks.

THE OUTLAW

It's like what that rock and roll monster Bon Jovi said: "I'm a cowboy, on a steel horse I ride / I'm wanted dead or alive." Or how Charles Manson's followers cut a fetus out of that movie star's still-warm belly. No, not like that at all. More like Bonnie and Clyde falling in love and bank robbing and being like, "Fuck all y'all and all y'all's motherfucking rules." It's like bad guys who are really good guys on the inside, who can't help being essentially good but who also have to kill people sometimes or skin them alive—if and only if the other essentially bad people totally deserve it. Or maybe it's not like that. Maybe it's like Duke Mantee, Bogart's character in *The Petrified Forest*, finally letting loose and killing the effeminate poet played by Leslie Howard, who keeps saying, "Kill me, Duke," until Duke finally does kill him. It's like Clint Eastwood on the screen, not the boor he's come to play offscreen. It's like the idea of Jesse James but not the horror of Jesse James—massacring all those people in Lawrence, Kansas, with Bloody Bill Anderson, slaughtering hundreds of men and boys in cold blood. Or maybe it's exactly like that.

MAKES 2 COCKTAILS

Black hats, white hats, guitars, peacemakers, gats, tommy guns, heaters, horses, dames, bullwhips, schoolmarms, horse whips, heroin, Apple products, skateboards, surfboards, waterboards, motorcycles, tattoos, the dark web

Whiskey
Bitters
Sweet vermouth
2 cherries

CONTINUED

1   Put all the shit on the table and make a Manhattan. Don't say
     anything. Ever. Don't ever say anything again. If you're really as bad
     as you need to be, you're horrible. And if you're not that bad, you're a
     pretender. Sorry. You're stuck. You can't really be as good as you want
     to be if you're as bad as you want to be. Killing Bon Jovi isn't an option.
     Hole up in your hotel room and wait. Sip your drink. If you make this
     correctly, it won't end well, but cheer up. Someday somebody'll write a
     song about you.

VENISON AND BLACKBERRY PASTIES

For you and your dearest, venison pasties. We recommend getting the meat from a hunter, not the side of the road. If you can't find venison, substitute beef chuck.

MAKES 6 PASTIES

1 lard crust recipe (see the headnote for Pie School Pastry Crust, page 241) (substitute all-butter pie crust if lard isn't your thing)
1 pound venison chuck
¾ cup chopped onion
¼ cup chopped carrot
¼ cup chopped turnip
1 (6-ounce) waxy potato, sliced thin on mandoline
1 teaspoon fresh thyme or rosemary
¾ teaspoon sea salt
Heaping ¼ teaspoon freshly ground black pepper
1½ cup blackberries (fresh is best; frozen is fine)
Egg-white wash (1 egg white plus 1 teaspoon water, beaten)

1   Prepare the crust, divide it into six portions, cover tightly, and let it chill for at least 1 hour in the refrigerator.

2   Preheat the oven to 400 degrees F. Line a large baking sheet with parchment paper.

3   Using a sharp knife, chop the venison into small chunks. In a large bowl, mix the venison with the onion, carrot, turnip, potato, thyme, salt, and pepper. In a small bowl, smash the blackberries with the edge of a wooden spoon so they're about half jam, half berry (or, if you're using frozen berries, half berry shards, half whole berries), and then add them to the venison mixture.

CONTINUED

4   Retrieve one of the dough balls from the refrigerator, roll it out on a floured surface into a ⅛-inch-thick round, fold it in half, put it on a plate, and then place it in the refrigerator. Roll all the pasty crusts and store on this plate until you're ready to fill the pasties.

5   Place a rolled round of pastry on a flat surface. Scoop ½ cup of filling (and not more) from the bowl, and place the filling in a mound down the middle of the pastry round, leaving at least 1 inch bare on all sides.

6   Fold the pastry over so its edges meet, making a pocket of venison filling. Trim the edges so they're even (I use a pizza cutter), fold the edges over themselves about ½ inch, crimp them with a fork, add a few vents to the top of the pastry, and store it in the refrigerator on a plate or baking sheet until ready to bake all the pasties. Repeat with the remaining rounds of pastry.

7   Arrange the pasties on the prepared baking sheet. Brush the pasties with egg-white wash, sprinkle with a little kosher or sea salt (I do mean a little— it'll go a long way), and bake in the middle of the oven for 20 minutes. Reduce the oven to 325 degrees F and bake for 40 more minutes, turning the pan front to back halfway through to ensure even browning.

8   Let the pasties cool on a wire rack until they're cool enough to handle. Eat at any temperature, but warm is best. Wrap leftovers tightly, and store in the refrigerator up to 3 days.

Is it good? Sir, it is pie. It will bring to camp any idiot that sits in darkness anywhere.

—MARK TWAIN, "TO THE PERSON SITTING IN DARKNESS"

MEET ME IN THE BOTTOM

GARY COPELAND LILLEY

It is Friday night, the first in months
that I don't have to work, a janitor
in the long rooms of small cubicles.

I am the politely unseen.

Despite blackwater fishing, pies in the oven,
and barbeque, North Carolina is the postcard
that you hobo out of. And so tonight
my buddy Chris and I sing Lead Belly,
trance blues, gospel, and Woody Guthrie songs.

November is nothing but the promise of snow.

We are blued, tattooed, and neither of us
lately have been regular churchgoers
or drinkers, but here we are, the Maker's Mark
is on the table, a spirit in a jar, our holy war.

Behold, the blessed laborers have jobs.

Carolina is no warm spot in the winter;
an old man, a Vietnam vet, got shot
by a young addicted girl; bored cops
are dangerous, stay off the roads. I wonder
how it was before the devil was released.

Nobody here rides easy.

Guitars in hand, we are the low waged
who are not-to-be-messed-with tonight,
booze and a rebellion music in the static,
an older black man and a post-punk kid.

Take Carolina, and give it to the crows.

We huddle in front of the space heater
that keeps the front room warm.
Water pipes are bursting in Winston.
I leave a thin, cold stream flowing
from all the faucets to prevent freezing.

I need to get the cold out of my bones.

STRAIGHT NO CHASER

KRISTEN MILLARES YOUNG

BEING PREGNANT IS A beautiful thing. Don't rounded bellies and fulsome breasts give you a warm sense that all is right in the world? If not, seek therapy. Gestation is fundamentally good.

Or so everyone tells me. I've done many things I'm proud of—not enough, mind you—but never in my life have I garnered so much praise and congratulations simply for walking down the street. While there is beauty in feeling so revered, this admiration casts a long shadow.

As a woman, I've been subject to mighty pressures to conform. Be sweet, not angry. Don't furrow your brow, and if you do, paralyze your face before the lines cut too deep. Support others before you attend to yourself. Don't fret when men talk over you. Smile, hear them out, and offer a thoughtful response. Stay pretty as long as possible. Be glad to give up what you love for your children.

But I am loud, and I find myself scowling when I write or think or talk or do anything that requires focus. My abuela fears I'll never conquer my temper, and she's probably right about that. My family considers my husband to be a miracle simply because I possess a strong character.

And yet, I often buckle. There's power in numbers. To succumb to expectation gives access to privilege most people decline to discuss because they don't want anyone to notice how compromised they, too, have become. In other words, I get away with more when I'm dressed nice, and I got away with the most when I looked single. If you could only see my closet—so many dresses designed to showcase my "best features" and minimize any evidence of an unfeminine appetite for excess. Soon I won't have the time or energy to pull myself together, and I'll feel the full fall from social grace. I'm fine with that, I think.

In the realm of child-rearing, I deferred for years and have attempted to mitigate that risk by having two children at thirty-three and thirty-four, just eighteen months apart. Beyond thirty-five, there be dragons in the uterus, or so we're told.

As I've blossomed, soaked in the adulation of family and friends and strangers for whom I am perfect because I am procreating, I've realized how direly I've craved such approbation since childhood, and how its presence reveals what I've known all my life: that we withhold praise from one another on a daily basis.

Why should this be? What generosity of spirit resides, unspeaking, within so many, only to be unlocked by the sight of an uncomfortable woman waddling through her third trimester?

I'm the kind of person who says hello to everyone I pass. This small-town friendliness plays well in my diverse neighborhood, though I've found it alarms a certain sector of the population, people whose eyes search the cracks in the sidewalk if they don't have a phone in their hands. I smile regardless. Those who respond are often surprised at being addressed by a fellow human on the sidewalk. The best of them—like the old man who blessed me for picking up trash—start a conversation that continues.

Yet during my pregnancy, I've been astounded by the number of people who for the first time see our common humanity as reason enough to greet me. In the beginning, I was taken aback. Must I spawn to merit acknowledgment? After reflecting on these exchanges during the long months of gestation, I've come to see a higher truth. Until I decided to become a parent, these people did not think we shared enough experience to warrant a relationship. I became visible because my choices seemed to affirm their values. Which makes me sadder than I want to be while carrying a child inside me.

If only we could uncouple the bounty of our empathy from the performance of a common task.

While I have framed this potential in its negative light, I do believe that joining the parenting tribe has proven to me the possibility of human connection and shown me the closest thing I've seen to the divine.

Society demands to be born anew. Without an unceasing supply of children, no institution on earth, not even the economy, would survive, and so advocacy for procreation is relentless. By enacting reproduction, I create our collective future and serve, through my body, a vital function.

As usual, to correct for ills elsewhere, the system makes impossible demands of the worker. With the providence of fertility come expectations of purity that would shorten the life expectancy of any expecting mother.

What I wouldn't give for a goddamned whiskey. Y'all be careful about who you let slice your pie.

COOKING FROM SCRATCH

JUDY BLUNT

MY DAUGHTER WAS IN high school when it came clear to me just how different our lives were going to be. We were three teenagers and a single mom buzzing through a typical weeknight in Missoula, supper preparations, homework, and music practice all underway in various corners of our cramped rental house—the groan of Jason's big bass fiddle warring for space with the television that James insisted made him think better, the phone ringing every few minutes. Jeanette slowed to an idle in the doorway of the kitchen, a huge miscalculation for anyone who didn't want to be put to work. Busy at the stove, I asked her to wash some lettuce for a salad and gave her some general directions for where to find it. She rummaged around in the crisper and came up with the head of iceberg, and soon I heard the rush of water in the sink. I don't know what made me stop what I was doing at the stove and look up. Maybe a waft of dishwashing detergent triggered my early-alert system. In any case, I caught her arm just as she prepared to plunge a fresh head of lettuce into a bath of hot soapy water.

Are you KIDDING me?

I suppose I yelled, though I was less angry or even surprised than I was simply, totally amazed. Wasn't the knowledge of such things as washing a head of lettuce inborn, part of our DNA, one of the reasons we were allowed out of the primordial soup and handed an apron? She responded like any reasonable, intelligent young woman who's been called to task unfairly—a little miffed, a little defensive. *Well you TOLD me to wash it.* Obviously, if I had any druthers about HOW it got washed, I should have spoken up.

As an adult, Jeanette still isn't much interested in the science of cooking, but she appreciates good food. In my job teaching at university levels, I find a lot of young people, male and female alike, who are pretty proficient at keeping themselves fed but who don't really cook. It's not that they can't, certainly, and I predict many will turn a corner at some point and find themselves staring at another wedge of frozen pizza or bowl of fluorescent mac and cheese and decide to take up the saucepan purely out of self-preservation. What makes me smile is the choice they have. They can cook or not, pick it up on the weekends and set it aside when it's not convenient. They can eat reasonably healthy foods three times a day and never soil a stockpot or wear out a paring knife. Cooking old-school looks like magic now.

How do you do that so fast? my son Jason asks, pulling up to a hot breakfast. There's a bit of wonder in his voice. He's home on leave from the army and pretty patient with my attempts to feed him up, given how much time he'll spend working it back off. Yesterday, I gathered some Braeburns, a couple of Galas, and a Granny Smith to make his favorite caramel-apple pie. This morning, breakfast has appeared in the time it took him to shower and pack his shaving kit. I do love a timed event. For me it's like dancing. I hear that first chord with a spark of joy and recognition, and fall into a rhythm I've known since childhood. Ingredients in one sweep through the refrigerator.

Potatoes scrubbed and grated, peels and all, and put to soak in cold water while pans heat, sausage links at a slow simmer in a little water. Potatoes wrung dry, dry, dry in a clean kitchen towel, spread in hot butter and olive oil, onion, a little green pepper diced and tossed in with salt and pepper. Lid whipped off the sausage pan and onto the potato pan, meat already steamed through starts to brown and sizzle as the last water evaporates. Slice the bread, set the table, pour some juice, flip the potatoes crisp side up, onion side down, then roll the sausage to another side and another side, and out to drain on a clean paper towel. And clean the pan. And back to low heat, a dot of butter, melting, check the spuds. Two eggs side by side, maybe three? Punch the toaster, grab the butter knife, take a minute to wipe up counters and put things away. When the toast pops, plate the spuds and eggs, sausage like punctuation, a hot meal in quotes. Buttered toast on a small blue plate. Stick a spoon in the jam jar, late-summer raspberries preserved for this moment. Pour coffee, two cups.

I sit with him while he eats. I'm well aware that this dance has nothing to do with sustenance. It's about love. It's about the tiny window of time we have before he boards another airplane for another war zone for another spell of months or years. I want him to leave my house full of old comforts. It's all I can do. As a ranch kid I learned about this sort of thing, the rules that go with mothers and food. If a calf or colt becomes separated from its mom, it will automatically return to the last place it fed. Always. Working with cow-calf pairs during branding or moving pasture was all about understanding that instinct. Trail them slow to keep them together, and if they're sorted into separate corrals for branding, make sure they mother up before they're turned out in a new pasture. The minute they feel lost, calves will leave the herd and climb through a dozen fences to get back where they came from. The place where they woke that morning, the spot they last suckled. The cows will pace the first fence, bawling. They can't climb through like their slippery little calves did, but they know right where to go when you open the gate. They line out in a high trot toward a mother-and-child reunion in the shelter of a grassy coulee umpteen miles back down the trail.

But with grown sons, some analogies are best left unshared. We talk small talk. I muse over my coffee as Jason scrapes the last of the egg onto the last bite of toast. He's grown into a big man, thick through the shoulders and chest, six feet three inches of lean muscle and precision. At thirty-two, he's an army captain, a Black Hawk pilot with the first dust of silver in the buzz of his sideburns; he's seen more of the world than I knew existed at his age. But the way he smiles has never changed, and now he leans back and pats his stomach. He's wise enough to know what I can't say, and we let each other be. *You know where to find me. Come back when you can. Come back home.*

THREE ROADS TO THE HEART OF IOWA

KATE LEBO

1.

FOR THE PAST FIVE YEARS I've spent the choicest three weeks of summer and thousands of dollars making pilgrimages to Iowa. One year I thought I'd go to Rome to study poetry. Then I met a woman on the internet who needed help baking pies in the American Gothic House, about two hours south of Des Moines. I'd make my bed in the parlor of the house that immortalized rural America. So what if I had to roll a hundred crusts in hundred-degree heat? Rome could wait.

The next year, a ticket to Des Moines from where I was working in upstate New York cost $137 more than a ticket to Rome from that same location. In addition to the Iowa State Fair's famous butter cow, a statue of Kevin Costner would be carved in twenty-five pounds of butter before my very eyes if I got there soon enough, *and* I could help judge the Machine Shed Pie Contest. Rome could keep waiting.

The year after that I didn't pretend I was going anywhere other than Des Moines, but I added a twist: I'd drive there with my partner from our home in Spokane, Washington.

Once you're miles deep in southern Idaho or eastern Montana or western Nebraska or anywhere in Wyoming but the Grand Tetons, you realize that this is how a person travels when she's been reared on eternity-long Catholic masses followed by ambrosia and pancake feasts at the Old Country Buffet. I trust gratification that's earned; in the interest of being gratified, I'll pursue a way to earn it. So what's Sam's excuse? To find the worn-out heart of America, he says, you have to take the long way.

I am, right now, in fact, writing in Omaha instead of Berlin, resting from this summer's pilgrimage in an Airbnb where the sound of traffic to the Old Market sounds like an ocean view someone else is paying for. I am in Omaha, hiding from my relatives (forgive me Aunt Lisa) before continuing the fifteen hundred miles home, because true shelter is being near family without having to talk to them.

It would have been different if it weren't for pie.

I received the craft according to modern ritual: after an uninterested childhood and aborted early-adult attempts to learn from books, I asked my mother to teach me. Why yes, it happened to be Thanksgiving.

Mom was born and raised in northcentral Iowa, near the Loess Hills, which gives her natural authority regarding anything baked, farmed, or otherwise related to Eden-grade topsoil, modesty, and hard labor. Even if she used to think she was bad at this pie stuff, and even if she is now a strict kale eater who avoids all desserts except ice cream, pie remains her birthright. As an Iowan, she was perfectly equipped to pass it down to me.

Not that she bragged about or even believed this pedigree. The way she saw it, pie's star turn at the holiday table meant that failure, should it occur, *would be noticed*. Especially by my paternal grandmother, whose limited cooking prowess (vodka tonics and Christmas Jell-O) did not prevent her from commenting on the culinary efforts of others (favorite memory: Grandma L shoves her pie plate away and pronounces my latest recipe test "TERRIBLE. Just terrible"). Mom handled her performance anxiety by expecting disaster, which she handled by maintaining a calm exterior while internally cataloging all possible catastrophes and a backup plan for each.

With our first pie, things did go wrong. The dough tore when we tried to get it into the plate, it wouldn't crimp neatly, we couldn't even begin to summon the courage for a real top crust. When I teach today, the same shit happens; something always goes wrong. It's either too hot in the kitchen or not cold enough in the fridge, or the oven is too full, or I've forgotten the egg, or I didn't buy enough butter, or we're short on blueberries, or someone has hot hands and will never, so help them God, make good pie crust. I try to strike a balance of being encouraging but realistic with these people. "You have hot hands, don't you?" I'll ask when I see the telltale signs of a dark, mushy dough. "One in six of my students has hot hands," I'll say. "Run them under cool water and work fast." This trick does not work as well as I want it to, but I have to tell them something.

One student in every class will have a hard time of it no matter what I do; I know this. Yet when I teach, I am awash in anxiety for not completely controlling the elements to ensure everyone's success. This is why, like a good lapsed Catholic, I start each class with a confession. "When my mother taught me about pie," I say, "she taught me to expect anything to go wrong at any time."

And isn't preparing for disaster a larger lesson mothers pass down to daughters? If Mom's love for her children is studded with shards of worry she couldn't help picking up on her steady and sensible way down motherhood's road, then all my pies are shaped in deference to and as a rejection of that lesson, a way of handling the possibility of disaster while ignoring it entirely, which is the same way we handle actual disaster: with jokes, despair, a well-stocked buffet, and hope—we won't quite call it faith—that the oven can heal all.

2.

I have never been served funeral pie at a funeral. I have eaten miniature lemon-meringue pies, stacks of chocolate-chip cookies, coffee cake hunks of indeterminable variety and inestimable age, but not what I am told is a German or maybe Amish tradition of funeral pie, also known as rosina pie, also known as sour cream raisin. Perhaps I haven't been to enough funerals.

It's a sweet made by farm mothers to trick their children into eating spoiled cream, said the second-prize winner at the storytelling contest I host for the Iowa State Fair. I think of fruit as a symbol and reward of the passing seasons, which makes raisins—dried grapes that have refused to rot—stopped time.

From what I can tell by the scant writing that exists about sour cream–raisin pie, it's called funeral pie because it's made with ingredients that are available year-round, which was handy in prerefrigeration days when someone croaked in January. The Iowans I've met who fondly remember it insist that funeral pie can't be properly made without a cow. Fresh cream gone bad, not store-bought stuff that's just as comfy lumped on top of a hot beef sundae.

I know a few farmers, but none who have a cow, so it's impossible for me to taste this dish in its correct context: made on the fly to use up old cream, or made for a funeral because Granny couldn't wait for peach season to meet her maker. You could call funeral pie a dying recipe.

Outside of a contest that encourages people to tell their pie disaster stories, only the brave compete at the Iowa State Fair with sour cream–raisin pie, and the only clear invitation for it comes from the Machine Shed Pie Contest, a massive competition that pits twenty-five divisions of pies—Lattice Top Cherry, Apple Crumb, Pumpkin (one crust), Pie Other Than Named (any crust can be used)—against their brethren before advancing the winner of each division to the grand-prize round. That's when judges go behind a curtain to duke it out: Chocolate Silk goes head to head with Strawberry Rhubarb, which goes head to head with Pineapple Cream, which competes with Sour Cream Raisin, which can't last a round against sexier, sunnier treats.

My first close encounter with funeral pie was in front of an audience. At the Iowa State Fair, food judging mostly takes place before a gathered crowd of competitors and supportive (or footsore) supporters who sit in folding chairs, chatting among themselves in the air-conditioning while the ladies and gentlemen of the jury take their sweet time to properly judge each entry.

That first time at the fair, still an outsider, I was assigned the pies no one else seemed to want: gooseberry, rhubarb, and sour cream raisin. "What is sour cream raisin?" I asked Ruth, my notetaker.

"Just be glad you didn't get mincemeat," she said.

My first bite was underwhelming. "Library paste" is how Jen Bervin and Ron Silver of *Bubby's Homemade Pies* describe it. They weren't far off, though the description probably has more to do with the beige hue of the filling and heavy cornstarch texture of some versions than with any whiff of actual glue. In other words, the pie was fine. One of those slices that doesn't knock you out but would comfort in a pinch.

Sour cream–raisin pie could even be a perfect symbol of the Iowa State Fair—modest materials presented for this civic occasion as grandly as possible, tarted up and shown off in a culture where demanding attention tends to be frowned on, punished with gossip, and condemned as self-interest at the expense of the community. "For those New York types, something's got to be in it for them," said one of my fellow judges. "Are you East Coast elite or West Coast elite?" a dry-humored rector asked before I taught a pie class in the basement of his Decorah Lutheran Church. "West Coast," I said, "but my parents are from Iowa."

When you sign up to judge the fair, no one gives you a manual for how to judge or what to expect, so I shut up and watched, and pretty soon figured out that all the power in that place is held by the grandmas. Arlette Hollister in particular and most obviously, being the superintendent of the Food Department, but also distinguished pie ladies like Dianna Sheehy of Audubon, Iowa, who's won so many ribbons she's been promoted to judgeship. Dianna liked my dresses and let me hang out with her, but the Iowa State Fair is one place where you can't just show up in a cute outfit and expect to be taken seriously. You have to put in your time. You have to be nice. You have to come back, and keep coming back, until people greet you with recognition instead of curiosity, which around here is sometimes just a polite way to look suspicious.

You're probably wondering by now, so I'll tell you: if you want to bake a prizewinning sour cream–raisin pie, be aware of these five dangers.

First among them is the liberal use of spices, particularly cloves. This pie is supposed to be heavily spiced—perhaps as a reminder of times when we masked rotten tastes with sugar and spices—but not so much that the filling tastes like a mouthful of essential oils. Cloves are particularly assertive when too concentrated, and more noticeably off when old, so get a fresh jar and don't use more than a quarter teaspoon.

The second danger is a soggy bottom crust, which can be solved by freezing the unfilled, unbaked crust for at least ten minutes before filling it. Completely frozen crust works well, too, but is not as ideal for reasons science has yet to determine. I'm guessing that putting frozen dough in a hot oven mutes the minute puffs of steam that occur early in the baking process and create flakes. These details can be forgotten in home baking, but if you intend to win a blue ribbon at the Iowa State Fair, remember where the devil is.

Third, the filling must not be too cloyingly sweet. Reduce the sugar content in the filling of any given funeral pie to one cup total, no more. Serve this pie cold, if possible. The cream, spice, and dried fruit get along better if they've had some time to chill.

Forth is meringue, which I enjoy eating but avoid making and so cannot command authority to help you here. I can tell you that the blue-ribbon winner had a nice, evenly browned pile of it on top of his or her entry and that it perfectly balanced the heavier flavors below.

Fifth, be hair aware. My first bite of funeral pie at the Iowa State Fair remained connected to its slice by a silver strand of hair, so bright and so long that the front row gasped and sprang back as I brought the bite to my mouth. *Is there a SPIDER in my pie?* I thought, then saw the hair, picked it off, slung the bite in the garbage, spun the offending dessert 180 degrees, sliced a new triangle, and sampled that, mustering the best stone face I could for the benefit of the baker, who was almost certainly one of the horrified people in the audience. In my judging notes, I covered the hair in a feedback sandwich, written in beautiful cursive by Ruth: "Lovely presentation. Hair in pie, unfortunately—would be a good idea to tie back hair when baking. Rich buttery crust, could have been slightly more salty but overall yummy." Quality of Crust (flavor and texture): 27 out of 30; Filling (flavor, consistency, appearance): 22 out of 30; General Appearance: 20 out of 25; Originality: 15 out of 15, minus 15 points for the hair, for 69 out of 100 overall points. "They really appreciate the feedback," Arlette assures us. I wanted mine to say this pie was a disaster, yes, but don't worry. At the Iowa State Fair, there's always next year.

As I progressed through my sour cream and raisin feast—a bite from the tip to test filling, a bite from the end to test crust, two bites for only the best pies—I did not grow to love sour cream raisin so much as start to understand what it offered: this is a pie that tastes best once it's been wedded by memory to the circumstance of its serving. A funeral lunch, let's say, where the mourners are all cried out and ready to swap funny stories about their dead. I remember watching my uncle at his wife's funeral lunch, at the head of the head table with his daughter and son, their partners, their kids, him the fifth wheel, the uncoupled, presiding over us as he had at his wedding. He didn't have much of an appetite that day but kept his seat until lunch was done. After the salads and sandwiches and soup, we were served something sweet that didn't demand attention, a brownie or cookie or something like that—I can't remember. It would have been the perfect time for funeral pie, except the name was perhaps too dark, too directly referential of the ritual we were about to finish, too much a reminder that when this was all over, we'd have to return to daily lives where loss is not so easily accommodated. To expect a swoon-worthy performance of every sweet is to expect too much of sweetness. Sometimes dessert needs to soothe, not dazzle. Moving on is wrenching. Sugar helps.

3.

It wasn't really delight on my grandmother's face, but she *was* weirdly cheerful considering we were at my cousin's funeral. "In my day we would have hushed a suicide up," she said. "But look at all these people!" She'd wrapped her hair in a plastic hood, her out-of-the-house 'do since time immemorial, so I couldn't tell how white her hair had gone since I'd last seen her. While we milled around the grave, hugging and crying and watching my cousin's wife, Christina, for a break in composure, Grandma wove between me and my brother, dry-eyed, happy we'd come home.

It was the autumn after my first pilgrimage to the Iowa State Fair. I hadn't stopped to see her that summer, but she didn't know that or care, my days as opaque to her as hers were to me. I didn't stop, because Carroll is a two-hour detour and not on the way to Omaha, not like Grandma insists it is when she wants one of her kids to pick her up, and talking to this grandmother has rarely been easy. When I imagine her life, it's in a soft chair across the room from the big-screen TV that is her company and her clock, passing her old age a doorway's distance from the room where my grandfather died. She's not ready to join him but only truly comfortable when couched in this purgatory, the three-bedroom house bought new in 1952 when she was pregnant with her first of seven.

We bridge our distance with pleasantries—it's hard for me to pin her down with anything else—so I'm surprised and sort of proud she'd acknowledge the reason for this funeral at the actual funeral. Then again, Phyllis has always said crazy things she may or may not believe, her conversational leaps and gaps hard to follow because their purpose, I think, isn't what she says, but the whirring of her worry beneath. "I wish they'd invent something to put all the water in the East on the West and take out the forest fires around your house," she said, which probably meant *I love you.*

We hadn't planned on being near Breda, Iowa, in the coldest part of October, or on wearing our good shoes and dark clothes in the field where we bury our dead, but here we were, my cry-easy clan of folks who feel most at ease with a job to do, trying our best to parse the short version of an awful story. A couple weeks after his twenty-ninth birthday, my cousin shot himself with his hunting rifle. He'd had another fight with Christina. She'd gone upstairs, where their little girl was sleeping, and refused to come down. He'd gone to where his gun was.

Matt's blood alcohol level was .25 or .29; the story changes, but these details—remembered now as wishes—stick: If only he'd had one more drink and passed out. If only he hadn't been preparing for a hunting trip. If only we'd known how to help him.

There is a long version of this story. To hear it, you'll have to ask Christina.

Because he died young and suddenly, with no will or end-of-life plan but with plenty of time for his wife to move someplace and start over, my cousin was buried next to his mother, possibly in the spot they'd set aside for his father. My uncle, his dad, was widowed young, too, and who knows where his final resting place will be. With his second wife, I would think, though Bill still writes "Remember Amy" in family wedding books, right underneath the *and* between his and Carol's names.

How do you prepare for a day like this?

There were lemon-meringue pies at the funeral lunch. Little minis so we would not have to share.

I wore a beige dress because I didn't own a black one.

My brother Nick wanted to see Matt one last time, so our family asked for a special viewing after the wake.

He was all made up in his volunteer firefighter suit, pretty spiffy except for the slackness of his face, the horrible, almost-concealed collapse of him. I cannot tell you about the sound my mother made or what my brother was thinking, but I can say that when we left the funeral home, for the first time in memory, Dad asked Nick to drive.

The graveside ceremony where Grandma joined us was easier. That's when our elders arrived, the great-aunts who couldn't travel. I met Arlene and Millie for the first time and saw that as I kept my promise to my mother ("Don't die before I do"), I would look first like Mom and then like her aunts. Arlene liked that Nick was a lawyer. When I told her I was a writer, she gave me the benefit of the doubt. There were final words from the priest, a splash of holy water, a folded flag bestowed on Christina by Matt's squad. We were still gross with curiosity and grief, still watching her for a clue, but we were beginning to understand we'd never get one. That it might not be our clue to get.

I do not know if going to Red's Place after a funeral is a family ritual or if, given the sudden and violent circumstances of our reunion, we all just needed a drink. Grandma had a standing date with the five o'clock news, so we kissed her good-bye at the cemetery. "I wish they'd put all the water in the East on the West," she said again. "I know, Grandma," I said. "Me too."

The bar is a blur.

I remember feeling right at home, the glow of a clean dive and a long curve of solid wood with secret Prohibition drawers, installed when nearby Templeton was getting its reputation for rye. I remember the poker table in back, one of many where my grandfather would sit and laugh with friends before he won their money. A perfect bar to get afternoon drunk with your family on a day that needed to hurry up and end.

We filled the biggest table in the room. Matt's brother and father and stepmom, cousins, their parents and siblings, our black and beige clothes, suit jackets slung over chairs, purses agape on the floor, Mom with her club soda, Dad and Nick with pints. Me, I walked up to the bar like I knew what I was about, or was trying to, like maybe I lived here a long time past, or like all dives are the same before sundown, everyone's place when they badly need one, a hometown for strangers. I ordered a whiskey rocks, Bud Light back. I put them on my father's tab. When I returned to the family table, we were almost all there, not quite ready to propose a toast but prepared for what a day like this required.

HOMECOMING

JACOB H. FRIES

A HUNDRED FEET ABOVE the water, on a grassy bank overlooking the Spokane River, I stood in the August sun swirling my glass. I drank whiskey then—I drink it now—because Mom told me to. When I was going away to college, I asked her what a good, respectable man's drink was. A single mother of us three boys, she was as much a man as I'd ever met.

"Whiskey," she said. "Neat or on the rocks. A beer or water back. Good for all occasions."

Mom herself preferred vodka, sometimes with Kahlúa and cream, always with a vanishing pack of Kool Milds within reach. That's one of my first memories of her: cigarette ash, swirling around her head as she drove, coating every surface in the car, glazing the windows in a green-gray grease. I'd write my initials on the glass. Then I'd draw messages backward, better for people in passing cars to read.

Mostly because it was short, I always wrote the same two words: "Help Me!"

"Very funny," Mom would say. "Always the clever one."

I was the oldest by ten years, which, in a way, made me Mom's longest-running relationship. Before she met Bob the bartender, and before my two kid brothers came along, it had just been us. She hustled tips at a Chinese restaurant in a strip mall in the valley. At night we dined on microwaved hot dogs or mac and cheese. On weekends, lacking a television, we'd stay up late listening to records and dancing.

When I was sixteen—after Bob left for the last time—Mom dropped the boys with a neighbor and took me to dinner at a downtown hotel as my reward for straight As. She bought herself a new dress and me my first necktie. We ate escargot and steak. I had Shirley Temples with maraschino cherries; Mom had martinis straight up. It was the happiest I had ever seen her.

"You're going to get far away from here, have fabulous adventures, and do *great* things," she told me.

Basking now in the summer sun, I wasn't so sure. I watched as my brothers—barefoot, pressed slacks rolled to their knees—tiptoed back and forth on the dirt switchbacks, down the bank, toward the river. John, the eldest at fourteen, carried the cardboard box, and little Ben obediently followed.

On the overlook, I inched my feet farther apart, imagining how good, respectable men stood, and lifted my drink.

"Keep going!" I called down to the boys.

They waded into the river, which, this time of year, was more like a creek, four or five feet at its deepest.

I shouted again: "Go all the way to the middle!"

After her second DUI, with the threat of jail time, Mom stopped drinking altogether. Everyone had a certain allotment of drinks, she said, and she had used up hers. Things changed quickly then: We stayed up nights studying together, me with US history, her with freshman-level community college courses. She drained cans of Diet

Coke like she was on some caffeine-fueled bender, stacking up fallen soldiers at the end of each day.

She said she wanted to be a teacher, maybe a social worker.

"You'll do *great* things," I told her.

When I left for college on the other side of the state, Mom nearly had enough credits for her associate's degree.

When the hospital administrator called me four years later, Mom had finished her bachelor's and was enrolled in a master's program at Eastern, starting that fall.

When I sat in the hard plastic chair at her bedside, I knew that was all over.

"Help me," she said. "Finish the job I couldn't. Take care of the boys. Do that for me, please."

She didn't have to tell me what to do with her. I knew enough to take her home.

Hip deep in the river, John handed the cardboard box to Ben, whose little arms held it steady as John pulled out the plastic bag from inside. He tore a hole in one corner and, grabbing the other end of the bag, raised it over his head, triumphantly.

Thick ash and shards of bone slid out, forming a dense cloud in the emerald water. The boys stood still as the current slowly stretched the ash into a twenty-foot-long gray ribbon, gliding over pools and snaking around rocks.

I traced the journey in my head: the Spokane, to the Columbia, over the Grand Coulee, down to the Tri-Cities, past Hanford, over to Portland, out to the Pacific, then maybe Hawaii or the Philippines. There was no destination, no end.

"You're going to get far away from here and have fabulous adventures," I said.

Watching the ribbon slide out of sight, becoming the river itself, I emptied my glass.

THE SACAGAWEA SOUR

Everybody loved Lewis because he was beautiful and insane and his first name was Meriwether. Clark was the problem. They were both problems, actually. But Clark would *refresh the men with a glass of whisky after Brackfest*, then charge John Collins *with getting drunk on his post out of whiskey put under his Charge as a Sentinel and for Suffering Hugh Hall to draw whiskey out of Said Barrel*. Let me tell you something about Hugh Hall: he was not suffering anything that morning—until Clark whipped him while Lewis lay weeping in his tent. The problem was that neither of these idiots could ever shut up. They were always handing out flags, accusing people of mutinous expression, and making speeches no one could bear to hear, though sometimes a group would feign interest just to keep them talking until their throats bled. They were awful spellers, too, used all kinds of random capitalization, and they wanted to name everything they saw as if nothing had been seen or named before. *I call this island Bad Humered Island*, Clark would say, and I'd think, *I call this island Asshole Island*. While Clark was having people whipped, Lewis was getting high and looking at plants and animals, smelling everything he touched, then looking at his hands and sniffing his fingers again. It was a long trip is what I'm trying to tell you. The idiot Clark would not stop calling me Janey. I was like . . .

CONTINUED

MAKES 2 COCKTAILS

Whiskey	Bitters	8 fluid drams laudanum
Sweet vermouth	2 cherries	

1   Just make the drink, okay? You know how. It's a Manhattan, all right? Sit at the table. Look at the laudanum. Sip your drink. Say this under your breath every once in a while: *Corps of Discovery.* Shake your head. Smell your fingertips. Sip your drink. Imagine the idiots whipping each other to pieces. Say it again: *Corps of Discovery.* Scoff. Mutter. Sniff your fingertips. Drink. Promise yourself never to lead anyone anywhere ever again.

FUNERAL PIE

Some people remember their granny making this pie with raisins only, and some remember it as sour cream and raisin with a layer of meringue. I found a recipe that calls for a raisin layer with a vanilla pudding layer on top, and another asked me to chop the raisins in a food processor so they'd make a smoother custard. All attempts to gussy up this pie failed to make it taste better. The best recipe is Judy Blunt's grandma's. Here there's no need for two layers—just let gravity sink the raisins to the bottom of the pie—and the raisins are simply spiced. To imitate fresh sour cream (which should be considered an oxymoron), I substitute homemade crème fraîche here. It's incredibly rich and easy to make, and it makes the pie better. Judy recommends making this recipe in an old-fashioned nine-inch pie plate, not a deep-dish pan.

MAKES ONE 9-INCH PIE

1 cup (8 ounces) heavy cream, the freshest you can find

2 tablespoons full-fat yogurt or buttermilk

½ recipe Pie School Pastry Crust (see page 241)

2 eggs

¾ cup sugar

1 teaspoon vanilla extract

½ teaspoon ground cinnamon

¼ teaspoon ground cloves

¼ teaspoon ground nutmeg

Pinch kosher salt

1 cup raisins

1   In a medium jar (a 12-ounce Ball jar would be perfect), make crème fraîche by combining the cream and yogurt and setting the jar in a warm place for 24 hours. About halfway through this time, shake the jar. After 1 day it should be thick and ready to go. If it isn't, leave it in that warm place for 1 more day.

CONTINUED

2   Prepare the dough and refrigerate it for at least 1 hour or up to 3 days.

3   Roll out the crust on a floured surface and place it in a 9-inch pie plate. Trim and fold the edges into a ridge. Flute the edges. Freeze the crust while you prepare the rest of the pie.

4   Preheat the oven to 375 degrees F.

5   In a medium bowl, combine the crème fraîche and eggs until smooth, then add the sugar and mix until smooth, then add the vanilla, cinnamon, cloves, nutmeg, and salt and stir to combine. Add the raisins, and stir to combine. Remove the pie plate from the freezer, and pour the filling mixture into the bottom crust, coaxing the raisins all over the bottom with the back of a wooden spoon to make sure they're even.

6   Bake the pie for 30 to 35 minutes or until the top of the pie is brown and the center stays firm when you jostle the pie.

7   Cool the pie on a wire rack. Do not serve until it is room temperature. This pie tastes best cold, and it tastes even better the next day. Store overnight in the refrigerator, covered with foil, for up to five days.

We ought to make
the pie higher.

—GEORGE W. BUSH

HUNGER FOR PIE, DREAM OF WHISKEY

M. L. SMOKER

Or was it dream of hunger/pie for whiskey?
However it goes, you have to want it and want it bad.
You have to show up in the middle of the night,
fork in hand, arms ready to raise another glass in solidarity
for all things sweet and treacherous in the world.

We must remember to savor the little joys in perilous times.
We are, after all, the right people for the job.
The ones who observe, watch, catalog, document, note,
describe, retell, create. We are alive and drunk in the world
and in our humble margins one might just find that which is worthy.
Take pie, for instance—so often overlooked,
disregarded, left off the menu entirely.
Yet, with delectable poise, it can show up unannounced

and the entire temperament shifts. Eat and dream of long summer
evenings, picnic tables, waning light, and the delicate taste of joy.

And then, don't forget the whiskey. Dangerous friend.
An eventual fall from grace in the making.
Neat, with water, on the rocks—but don't you dare think
of a mixer. Not tonight. Tonight's for the real, unadorned
partygoers. The truth-sayers, the lovers, the poets.

M. L. SMOKER

FRITO PIE

SHAWN VESTAL

IT'S TIME TO EAT, but Mom wants to talk.

"Name your favorite food," she orders, in a slurry, deliberate voice.

She has called us to dinner, my sister and I, and we arrive to find her sitting at the dining room table, blinds drawn, and nothing on the table but a fine pelt of dust and my mother's juice glass, half-full of amber liquid that looks like apple juice and smells like Listerine, and we have no idea what is going on, but something is certainly going on.

"Come on!" Mom growls. "What's your favorite food?"

It is not clear which one of us she's asking. My sister says, "Pizza," resentfully, and Mom slaps her hand on the table and shouts, "That's like saying your favorite food is *sandwich*!"

My sister says, "I have literally no idea what you're talking about."

My mother says, "Literally?" and takes a wincing sip from the glass, another sip that looks as if it is causing shooting pains in her face. She turns to me. "Buddy?"

"I guess pie," I say.

I am thinking of the chocolate-cream pies my sister buys with her Safeway money on Fridays after school when she gets her checks, the frozen chocolate-cream pies with whipped cream piped along the edges, which we eat straight from the pan, forks in hand, pie on the carpet between us, while we watch television in those wonderful, luscious hours before our parents return from work and begin orbiting in separate, angry spheres.

Mom stares at me contemptuously.

"What did I just say?" she asks. "What did I just say about pizza and sandwich?"

I try to remember. Everything seems to be happening behind a thick pane of glass. She breaks her stare, takes another face-hurting drink, and sucks air through her side teeth.

"You children," she says.

"Pie," she says.

My sister says, "Screw this," and scoots back her chair. Mom slaps the table again. "Sit down!" she says, and my sister, who never actually stood up, scoots her chair back in. Her obedience is astonishing, then frightening, because she never obeys.

Mom sighs heavily, as though she is exhaling all the mass of her body. "Whenever anyone tells me they like pie, they love pie, I always say, *Yeah? You like pie? Ever had Frito pie? Pie lover?*"

Strips of sunset are poking through the blinds, lighting up the hairy dust on the table. Mom stands, tips up her glass, and lunges into the kitchen. From the cabinet above the fridge, she pulls down a bag of Fritos, and from the lazy Susan under the counter she retrieves a can of chili. Fumblingly, she opens the chili and sticks it in the microwave, and my sister says, "You're not supposed to put metal in there," and Mom says, "Just who is the parent and just who is the child?"

The microwave sparks and smokes. Mom brings the bag of Fritos to the table and sets it facedown in the middle, ceremoniously, grandly, between us, her children, and she tears it open along the back seam, making a crinkly bowl of the bag. The smell of greasy fried corn wafts up into the scorched Listerine air. She puts on an oven mitt, reaches into the cupboard, and brings out a bottle of whiskey, splashes some into her juice glass and some onto the counter, puts it back, then opens the microwave and grabs out the chili, label blackened, carries it to the table—can in mitted hand, whiskey in the other—and upends it over the gaping bag.

Two drops of red liquid fall onto the curled tan chips. Mom says, "Holy jumping Jesus Christ," and a can-shaped cylinder of chili slumps onto the Fritos.

She hands us each a fork and says, "Dig in." My sister and I look at each other, and in that look we divide ourselves from everyone else in the world, Mom and Dad included, Mom and Dad especially. We cease—with that look—being unwitting about our station. We are prisoners, like the prisoners in *Hogan's Heroes*, and we will now begin our prisonerhood in earnest, unflaggingly, eyes open, with secrets and subterfuge and underground tunnels and microphones in the teapots and the cheerful, sustaining knowledge that someday we will be free, and until then, we will humor our captors.

"Where's Dad?" my sister asks.

Mom takes a heaping forkful of Frito pie into her mouth. Bits of chip and bean fall to the table. She says, "Gone to see a man about a horse," and snorts, bits of Frito pie flying into the Frito pie, and my sister says, with massive, glorious sarcasm, "He went to the bathroom?" and Mom says, "Never you mind."

She eats and eats. At some point, she begins talking, telling us a story, I think, but between the huge mouthfuls of Frito pie and the slurring, and then, eventually, the weeping, it is impossible to understand her.

MY YOUTH

CHRISTOPHER HOWELL

I'm still holding a girl's hand
by a fence in the dark schoolyard
after the dance class our parents insisted we attend.
Her blue dress still grazes my knuckle as we move
a little like dreamers, springtime softening
the little light there is.

I still believe if I touched her light
brown hair, I would be transformed, ennobled
by its luster
as Arthur was ennobled when Guinevere turned
that first time, and looked straight
into his eyes, the total clarity of that.

I'm still sneaking up stairs and out to walk miles
in the delicious loneliness of a night rain, walk past
the doomed berry farms and empty fields

and slouching Grange Hall, its one caretaker drunk again,
and, as I pass, holding up his arms, like always, a little
like Moses, that the waters part and spare us all.

He's still there, surely, if, walking backward, I could
undo the knots of cold disaster, the unremarkable days
that are so many. After all I'm still in canoes, baseball games,
fistfights, and drive-in movies with their huge, godlike screens
and sputtering speakers. Still having my first sip
of whiskey with Krueger up on Mount Tabor, getting too smashed
to stand.

Next day I'll be singing in the choir beside my father's
booming baritone, and thinking of that girl again,
the one who comes back in her blue dress
always, who holds my hand
without speaking, who dances with me all through
those years of tedious lessons, who looks
straight into my eyes.

THE THIRTEEN WONDERS OF TAMMY

SAMUEL LIGON

1. Niagara Falls

ONCE WE HAD SAVED two thousand dollars, we left home, and once we left home, we were never going back. My plan was to make Tammy happy forever. She didn't care about the wedding so much as the honeymoon, which would begin in Niagara Falls and last as long as the money held out, which would be as long as I kept gathering it. The Storybook Package included a carriage ride and two complimentary witnesses, plus a 20 percent discount at the Niagara Motor Lodge. Tammy loved that carriage, with a half bottle of champagne inside, and she loved the horses pulling it, Duke and Donna. She loved the *Maid of the Mist*, too, where we wore raincoats under the pounding spray, and she loved the stories the museum lady told us of daredevils plunging over the falls, smashed to smithereens, until Annie Taylor made a barrel out of oak and iron and survived. "A miracle!" the museum lady told us. "The woman who lived!" And Tammy said, "A miracle!" We watched the falls for hours after that, Tammy's hand in mine as the water roared around us.

2. Martha Washington's Pie

After the air conditioner broke in our rusted-out Lincoln, I pushed us through the heat of Indiana while Tammy read from a recipe card her mom had gotten from her mom, who'd gotten it from her mom, who'd gotten it from her mom, and all the way back to the mom who'd gotten it from Martha Washington. Tammy cherished that card, the one thing left of her mother and the mother of our country. But I wasn't so sure about a pie filled with turkey and sweetbreads and mullet and pigeons and oysters and partridges and suet and woodcocks—things you hardly even knew what they were—a half ounce of mace, a half ounce of pepper, six pounds of butter. "I don't think there's a pan big enough," I said, and Tammy got quiet again. The Lincoln's temperature needle ticked toward the red. We had a system for that—cranking the heat with our windows down, so that the road heat and the engine heat became one heat blasting all over us. Tammy took the cigarette from my hand and finished it in a swirl of smoke. "We'll find one," I said. But where would we find an oven big enough to hold it?

3. The Great Flour Mill Explosion

If there's one thing Tammy hated, it was gluten, and if there's one thing she hated more than gluten, it was the family farm. "They're ruining everything," she said as we drove past corn and soy and wheat and whatever else filled those endless fields. Tammy was a child of the Garden State, but she wouldn't eat from a garden. Or a farm. She wouldn't eat bread, either, or pizza, and she hated gluten-free food as much as she hated gluten. But she ate pie, gluten be damned. At the flour museum in Minnesota, we learned about the explosion of 1878, a spark igniting flour dust in the Washburn Mill and blowing the place to smithereens. Eighteen people died instantly, and more expired in the fires that destroyed the surrounding mills. We stood above the ruins along Saint Anthony Falls. The flour kings had rebuilt it all and were soon grinding three million pounds a day. "She won prizes and everything," Tammy said, and I said, "Who did?" and Tammy said, "She could've been the next Betty Crocker," and I didn't say anything, because sometimes Tammy just needed me to listen. We stood on a platform above the mighty Mississippi, and I thought, *Dough flow*, imagining a pipeline of molten butter joining a million pounds of flour pouring into the river to form our nation's crust. "My mother," Tammy said, "that's who," but I already knew.

4. Iowa

Tammy loved animals of every kind, cats and pigeons and hamsters and goats and donkeys and buffalo. Most of the West is a park of some kind—if not Yellowstone, Yosemite. If not that one, another one. There's thousands of them, filled with animals, and once we got out there, I'd become a park ranger, arresting the drunkards set on ruining the joys of nature for everyone else. Tammy would bring my supper to work in a cloth-covered basket, and after we ate, she'd stay to kiss me and pet the animals. There were all kinds of animals at the Iowa State Fair and giant things made of butter—a cow, the Empire State Building, things you didn't know why they were made of other things. We saw wriggling piglets and breeding-stock boars with enormous balls. We ate food on sticks and watched children ride sheep like rodeo riders. We walked through barns full of horses and rams, Tammy screwing up her courage to talk to the pie ladies in the food hall, the place her mother had won so many prizes as a girl. Tammy figured we'd bake a Martha Washington pie and become famous because we'd made such an awful, enormous thing, but none of the pie ladies were interested. They hated Tammy's feathered hair and fringed boots, her cutoff shorts and hummingbird tattoos. "Does anyone know," Tammy asked a panel of pie experts, "how much flour I'd need for a six-pound butter crust? Does a bushel seem crazy?" Nobody knew. I asked, "Does anyone even know how much flour is in a bushel?" but Tammy shushed me. None of the pie ladies wanted to be Tammy's mom or grandma. None of them knew of a pie pan big enough for Martha Washington's pie. I practiced the art of money getting in the judges' lounge but otherwise kept close to Tammy, loving her hard. Outside, it was a thousand degrees, and politicians stood on hay bales screaming.

5. The Electrical College

There's a famous college somewhere in Nebraska made of electricity, something Thomas Edison probably invented, something electrical, like that thing he did with the elephants on Coney Island that Tammy and I saw on TV, how he wired them and juiced them to prove a point about one kind of electricity being safe—his kind—and another kind being dangerous, the killing kind, smoke coming from the elephants' ears as they collapsed into smoldering heaps. Tammy cried in the humidity because the pie ladies hated her and Thomas Edison had fried those elephants for nothing. I harvested cash in the beer tent, the Iowans careless with drink. "Tell me about Martha's pie again," I said when we reconnected by the front gate, but Tammy didn't want to talk at all. "Look what I've been holding back," I said, fanning the cash I'd gathered. We had a party that night in a motel near Templeton, where they make the fancy whiskey. Sometimes money is enough.

6. The Corn Palace

Before he went away, my brother Kenny gave me a book our dad had given him, which our dad had inherited from his dad, called *The Art of Money Getting*, by P. T. Barnum, the famous circus boss. It's not just about money, either. It's a collection of wise sayings you can use in everyday life, such as "Be cautious and bold" or "Never have anything to do with an unlucky man" or "The history of money getting is the history of civilization" or "Many persons are kept poor because they are too visionary" or "You cannot accumulate a fortune by taking the road that leads to poverty" or "as Davy Crockett said, 'This thing remember, when I am dead: Be sure you are right, then go ahead.' It is this go-aheaditiveness, this determination not to let the 'horrors' or the 'blues' take possession of you, which you must cultivate." I shared passages with Tammy at night when we were resting against each other in bed. I did what I could to keep the "horrors" from taking possession of her. At South Dakota's Corn Palace, we looked at giant pictures on the walls made of corncobs, Elvis Presley and Willie Nelson, Ronald Reagan and Marilyn Monroe, corn cowboys and corn Indians worshipping corn elk and corn buffalo. Tammy said corn would only end up giving everyone diabetes. Her mother couldn't wait to get out of Iowa as a girl, couldn't wait to get off the farm. She was rescued and taken to New Jersey by a man she loved and then hated. But she knew how to make pie. Even as a girl. Tammy had seen the ribbons. After the old man went away she could have taken Tammy back to Iowa, but she stayed where she was, stuck. We weren't going to stay stuck anywhere.

7. Mount Rushmore

The amazing thing is how much those rocks really do look like human heads, a far cry from the constellations, beautiful in the Dakota night, but nothing like the archers and chariots we'd been promised back home, where only the moon and a glow from the Hess refinery flare stack can be seen in the Jersey night. Unlike those things that are supposed to look like other things but that really look only like themselves, the rocks of Mount Rushmore really do look like human heads. We stood beneath them after weeks on the road, gawking. Three men and a woman, it looked like, or two men and two women. We couldn't tell. Tammy had been sad and sadder, but now she said, "Do you believe these heads?" and I said, "It's a band is what it is," realizing this all at once. It was Rush, the band my brother Kenny had loved so much. But then we learned they were carved president heads. And then it seemed like Tammy would never stop crying.

8. Narcissa Todd Whitman

Everyone knows her as the first lady governor of New Jersey, but she was also the first white lady to cross the Rockies, a missionary and her missionary husband driving west in their wagon to save people, the same way we were headed west, though we knew we couldn't save anyone. The Whitmans should've known that, too, Tammy said. Everyone should know. Tammy knew everything there was to know about history, how the Whitmans went west, how they thought they could save Indians, how they got what they deserved—Marcus with a hatchet to his face and Narcissa shot a thousand times by the people she no longer even dreamed about saving. She was so happy early on, Narcissa. That was the tragedy. How she was happy and wanted to save people and then got unhappy and cared only about the white orphan children people like Daniel Boone kept dropping off. She and Marcus met lots of people on their long drive, and everyone was so shocked that a white woman governor from New Jersey was crossing the mountains when there weren't any roads or stores or churches or bars or anything else for white people. The Indians called the Whitman's wagon a land canoe. Narcissa was never happy in the West, especially after her baby drowned, but she had been happy before, when she thought there was a place where people could be saved—exactly the opposite of Tammy, who was going where she would be happy, knowing there was no one to save and leaving everything unhappy behind.

9. Massacre Rocks

Everything Tammy knows is so old and unlikely and far away, but everything we saw reminded her of those old, dead things. If it wasn't John Brown's body mouldering in the grave, it was the petrified man. If it wasn't the Mountain Meadows Massacre, it was the Sacking of Osceola. In Wyoming we stopped at Register Cliff, a place where the pioneers carved their names into rocks so Tammy and I could read them hundreds of years later, after the Oregon Trail had been transformed into a byway lined with gas stations and chain restaurants and affordable motels and dollar marts. The pioneers had walked all the way from the East—a long walk—and it made them furious. "They were desperate," Tammy said. She told stories about pioneers killing Indians and Indians killing pioneers and pioneers dressed as Indians killing Indians *and* pioneers, then stories about all the dead babies, and mothers run over by wagon wheels, and everyone sick and dying and miserable. "What about pie?" I asked her, and she said, "What about pie?" and I said, "Didn't they eat a lot of pie back then?" and she said, "What does pie have to do with anything?" and I didn't say anything. She wanted to stop at Massacre Rocks, and I promised we would, but she fell asleep from the road heat and engine heat, and I drove by without stopping. If you're not part of the problem, my brother Kenny used to say, you're part of the solution. It was the driest, most colorless country I've ever seen. I couldn't imagine walking across it.

10. The Ore-Ida French Fry Factory

The West makes you realize how much of the East is run-down and broken, but then you find a place like Ontario, Oregon, as run-down and broken as any town in New Jersey. Ontario is probably nothing like Kokomo—not the Kokomo in Indiana, but Tammy's Kokomo—though Ontario did have a french fry factory with a smokestack that blew perfect, gigantic smoke rings. From the highway we saw one floating over town, and we drove toward it. "Find it, baby," Tammy said. Another one floated up a few minutes later. Then another. It seemed like something magic would be under those rings. But it was just a giant french fry factory. It could've been special if we'd wanted it to be. A big old french fry factory blowing smoke rings. Way out in the middle of nowhere. A wonder.

11. Kokomo

Everybody knows a little place like Kokomo, but nobody knows it better than Tammy and I do. Sometimes that song looped in the Lincoln for hours, working its steel drum magic, its tropical contact high, as we navigated the blazing empty center of America in our land canoe. Sometimes it took hours, playing "Kokomo" seventy or eighty or a hundred times, but the song always brought us back to our love through its island beat and soaring saxophone solo, until we got to Portland, Oregon, which Tammy said was filled with hateful, horrible people. Weeks before, we'd driven through Maquoketa, Iowa, because Tammy thought it sounded like Kokomo. After that we went to Omaha, because she thought that sounded like Kokomo, too. We didn't know there was a real Kokomo in Indiana, named after Chief Kokomo, whose name means black walnut and has nothing to do with the Florida Keys or tropical drinks or Montserrat mystique. "Bermuda," I'd say to Tammy. "Bahama. Come on pretty mama."

But that didn't always work. She needed the song itself. She needed
the song over and over, sometimes for eight or nine hours straight,
until we got to Portland, so close to the very end of the country.
But that's not where Tammy wanted to go to get away from it all.
Even though she had a good piece of pie there. "Go the other way,"
she said. "I hate this place. All these Civil War veterans." We were
so close to the coast it seemed a shame, but I turned us around and
headed the other way, backward. I thought if she'd just see the ocean
where the Beach Boys were from, we'd settle down and start living
our lives. At the pie shop in Portland I asked the pioneer baker about
Martha Washington's pie, and she said maybe we could make one in
a washtub buried in the ground, covered and surrounded by coals. It
sounded brilliant. When I told Tammy about it, she shook her head
and started the "Kokomo" loop all over again.

12. Salt Lake City

There's a religion here that has to do with beehives and gulls and
grasshoppers and handshakes and magic underwear and love
planets. The men are supposed to have nineteen wives, or that's how
it used to be, which Tammy thought was awful, until she thought
it might be a good thing—a family having a spare somebody—just
because of the elephants and massacres and people smashing
themselves in barrels and her mother and flour-mill explosions and
how you could never be sure what would happen next. "No more,"
I said. "Please, Tammy." I held her and petted her. "California," she
said. I was happy we were headed west again, but Tammy was already
thinking of what she'd do next.

13. The Golden Gate Bridge

Which was jump, of course. She didn't know about the net, though—

what they'd put under the bridge to catch people like her. I didn't know about it either, the greatest wonder of them all, Tammy in a net under the bridge like a baby blown from a cradle in a treetop caught in another cradle under the one she'd just been blown out of. I lunged after her and watched her fall, then watched her get caught, her face showing surprise then joy, the happiest I'd ever seen her, Tammy laughing and laughing, the wind screaming and Alcatraz across the bay and water rippling everywhere around us. I climbed the rail and jumped after her to the basket below. It's amazing to fall like that, amazing to be saved. I thought of the rock and roll heads at Mount Rushmore and how one thing really could be like another— jumping off the Golden Gate like going over the falls in a barrel. The woman who lived! And Tammy was like, "Imagine a mountain of Led Zeppelin heads!" and I was like, "Yes, baby!" the wind howling around us in a basket under the Golden Gate Bridge, our hearts booming across mountains and rivers and rocks and plains, so many wonders out there waiting.

JUST A PIECE OF PECAN PIE
(& ALL I WANT IS YOU)

JOE WILKINS

MY GRANDMOTHER WAS A terrible cook. She burned on purpose good beef roasts to meaty strings. Fried lamp chops until the blackened bone was just about the tenderest bit. Considered boiled potatoes the star of any dinner. At her table creamed corn, sweet pickles, and crackers all counted as vegetables. And once she got it in her head to cook fish for Christmas Eve dinner. My mother, trying to be kind, mentioned that the salmon was nice. Dentures clacking, my grandmother revealed her secret: she had soaked the fish for half the day in bleach. "Gets rid of that fishy taste," she said, as she forked another bite.

He left many things behind, my father, when he died. A grieving wife, three young children, three hundred acres of drought-blasted farmland. And a host of teary, beer-drinking buddies who at every opportunity slung a thick arm over my thin shoulders and squeezed, told me once again—the words unraveling, ribboning off into nonsense—that I was the man of the house now. And in the dank basement, on the bottom shelf, below the canned beef tongue, below the headless stewing hens swimming each in its own half-gallon mason jar, my father left as well a white-and-red case of Rainier and three dusty bottles ambered with liquor, the liquid sliding like oil as in my hands I turned the bottles this way and that.

She could make a brown bread, though, that was crusty and dense and good, slicked with the strong white butter the neighbor woman churned and sold from her trunk after Sunday mass. She could make a rich fudge, too, midnight dark and sweetly bitter, studded with chopped walnuts. And when I close my eyes I can still taste my grandmother's sour cream and raisin pie. Like liquor, even the smallest bite of that pie filled the mouth with sharp, knotted flavors, a creamy vinegar, a sweet rot. And as if he knew just when, Johnny Ahern—a shirttail relation of ours, a sheep shearer and general roustabout—shows up in memory most every time my grandmother pulls a pie from the oven. Though I could only ever have one piece after dinner, Johnny got as many as he wanted. My grandmother tried to explain to me once about Vietnam; it still didn't seem right. Johnny'd work his slow way through a fourth slice, his fork moving as if underwater to his mouth, his face dark and wrinkled as a raisin. After he finished he'd wipe his greasy lips and lean back and roll a crooked cigarette, tap the ash into his hand. He'd grin at me. I'd glare back, check how much pie was left.

Winter midnight. A gravel road in the far, dry reaches. For the starshine our breath blooming before us. We were waiting, the idiot knot of hormones, boasts, and sadnesses we were, for my friend's father's hired man, who was supposed to meet us here at Bascom Creek, bring us a case of beer. He was one of those guys who drifts from small town to small town, either on the way to ruin from drink or rodeo or somehow odd, awkward—too religious, maybe, or artistic. This one was a heavy-metal drummer, claimed he'd recorded with a couple of bands back east. The artistic ones were often sought after by the local women, hungry for something different, yet it makes sense to me now why it never stuck, why these men instead paid such attention to us high school boys. When the hired man finally showed, he shrugged, told us he was sorry but the deputy was down from Roundup and cruising town. We spit, cursed, cut our eyes at him. He pulled a fifth from underneath the bench seat of his truck. Said we could all take a tug of his stash of Old Crow, if we wanted. It watered my eyes, but I held it down. Didn't even cough. The hired man drove off, and we stood there in the gravel beneath the thousand-thousand stars, cold and changed and trembling.

By the time my children met her, my grandmother had quit cooking altogether. She'd been going ever blinder for years—pockets of dry flour in the dark flesh of her bread, threads of her silver hair ribboning the crusts of her last pies—and had finally given in, let my mother do the cooking. On one of our last visits, she handed my wife a dark paper IGA sack with all her old pie tins—some rusting, some with holes in the bottom she didn't know were there—and she charmed my son and daughter with pocketfuls of saltwater taffy. They sat in her lap, and she pinched them and clucked at them and told stories, all the while slipping them bright taffies. She was ninety-four; they were three and not quite two. I figured the taffy was ancient, hard and stale, and on the walk back to my mother's place my son admitted that the taffies didn't taste very good, though he held them yet in his palm, held them up and out to me like precious stones, said, "But aren't they pretty?

What is best in us sits on the tongue. You taste the pure wild abandoned birdsong of a daughter's laughter. You lip like river rocks the salt of a gone father's hard hand. You stand the lonesomest animal in all those empty prairie miles and drink on the wind the dust and wild onion that was your grandmother. You taste and taste a lover. To be human is to grieve and eat. Nothing more. And nothing less. Each sip of whiskey the smoke of memory. The next bite of pie sufficient and essential, the one sweet thing.

THE PAT NIXON

Visitor to leper colonies. Outstanding Homemaker of the Year, 1953. Mother of the Year, 1955. The Nation's Ideal Housewife, 1957. First lady. Second lady. Tireless smoker. Daughter to a gold miner of Irish descent, born on Saint Patrick's Day Eve. Hence the luck. Hence the misfortune. Hence the fashion sense. "Pat doesn't have a mink coat," her husband said in that speech about their adorable dog he would not give up because he was such a good man. "But she does have a respectable Republican cloth coat, and I always tell her she would look good in anything." She did look good in anything. And everything. And nothing. Follower of Mamie and Lady Bird. Predecessor to Betty and Nancy, Pickles and Hillary. Presser of her husband's suits. "A paragon of wifely virtues," said the *New York Times*, "whose efficiency makes other women feel slothful and untalented." Epic pothead (unsubstantiated). Insatiable sexpot (unsubstantiated). Hater of animals (unsubstantiated). Baker of pies and distiller of whiskey (unsubstantiated). "He's very dear personally," she said of her husband. "I don't think I would have stayed with him otherwise." A woman of "good figure and good posture," according to *Women's Wear Daily*, with "the best-looking legs of any woman in public life today." It's true she preferred silence from the butlers and maids, but she also ordered the White House tour guides to allow the blind to handle the White House antiques during their insufferable, unending tours.

CONTINUED

MAKES 2 COCKTAILS

3 packs Tareytons
Don Gibson's recording
  of "Woman (Sensuous
  Woman)"

1 Republican cloth
  coat
Whiskey
Sweet vermouth

Bitters
2 cherries

1 You've been doing too much lately, beautiful. Housewife of the year,
   paragon of wifely virtues, presser of Dick's suits. Do you have any idea
   how special you are? I want you to open up another pack of Tareytons,
   baby, and make us another drink. Actually? I'll make the drinks. Then
   I'll put on that Don Gibson song "Woman (Sensuous Woman)" while
   you put on your Republican cloth coat and take off everything else.
   Let's drink our drinks and talk about what an asshole your husband
   was. Let's smoke a few Tareytons and see how your legs are holding
   up under all that mouldering. Let's silence the maids and butlers and
   posers up in Brooklyn trying to tell us how to make our drinks. Baby,
   let's float on cocktail and Tareyton fumes to that magical time when
   your husband was the most evil force we could imagine, scratching
   about like an adorable kitten in his litter box, trying so hard to cover up
   such small sweet nothings.

MARTHA WASHINGTON'S PIE

This is a recipe from *The Art of Cookery Made Plain and Easy: Which Far Exceeds Any Thing of the Kind Yet Published* by Hannah Glasse, originally published in 1747 and likely used by first FLOTUS Martha Washington to make her famous Yorkshire Christmas Pie. Caroline Kennedy's *A Family Christmas*, where we first encountered this recipe, attributes it to Martha, so we will, too. If anyone actually makes this pie, we will send them one pound of butter and one fifth of whiskey.

MAKES 1 PIE

1 First make a good standing crust, let the wall and bottom be very thick; bone a turkey, a goose, a fowl, a partridge, and a pigeon, season them all very well, take half an ounce of mace, half an ounce of nutmegs, a quarter of an ounce of cloves, and half an ounce of black pepper, all beat fine together, two large spoonfuls of salt, and then mix them together. Open the fowls all down the back, and bone them; first the pigeon, then the partridge, cover them; then the fowl, then the goose, and then the turkey, which must be large; season them all well first, and lay them in the crust, so as it will look only like a whole turkey; then have a hare ready cased, and wiped with a clean cloth. Cut it to pieces; that is, joint it; season it, and lay it as close as you can on one side; on the other side woodcocks, more game, and what sort of wild fowl you can get. Season them well, and lay them close; put at least four pounds of butter into the pie, then lay on your lid, which must be a very thick one, and let it be well baked. It must have a very hot oven, and will take at least four hours.

PIE SCHOOL PASTRY CRUST

This is the crust Kate taught in *Pie School: Lessons in Fruit, Flour & Butter*, and it's what she teaches still. Use it for any of the pies in this book that call for pastry. To make an all-lard crust, just substitute cold leaf lard (rendered, of course) for the butter in this recipe. It behaves very similarly and makes an incredibly flaky crust with just a slight whiff of the savory—perfect for the Venison and Blackberry Pasties on page 185.

MAKES 1 DOUBLE CRUST

2½ cups all-purpose flour
1 tablespoon sugar

1 teaspoon salt

1 cup (2 sticks) well-chilled
unsalted butter

1 Fill a spouted liquid measuring cup with about 1½ cups of water, plop in some ice cubes, and place it in the freezer while you prepare the next steps of the recipe. The idea is to have more water than you need for the recipe (which will probably use ½ cup or less) at a very cold temperature, not to actually freeze the water or use all 1½ cups in the dough.

2 In a large bowl, mix the flour, sugar, and salt. Cut ½- to 1-tablespoon pieces of butter, and drop them into the flour. Toss the fat with the flour to evenly distribute it.

3 Position your hands palms up, fingers loosely curled. Scoop up flour and fat, and rub it between your thumb and fingers, letting it fall back into the bowl after rubbing. Do this, reaching into the bottom

CONTINUED

and around the sides to incorporate all the flour into the fat, until the mixture is slightly yellow, slightly damp. It should be chunky—mostly pea-size with some almond- and cherry-size pieces. The smaller bits should resemble coarse cornmeal.

4   Take the water out of the freezer. Pour it in a steady thin stream around the bowl for about 5 seconds. Toss to distribute the moisture. You'll probably need to pour a little more water on and toss again. As you toss and the dough gets close to perfection, it will become a bit shaggy and slightly tacky to the touch. Press a small bit of the mixture together, and toss it gently in the air. If it breaks apart when you catch it, add more water, toss to distribute the moisture, and test again. If the dough ball keeps its shape, it's done. (When all is said and done, you'll have added about ⅓ to ½ cup water.)

5   With firm, brief pressure, gather the dough in 2 roughly equal balls (if one is larger, use that for the bottom crust). Quickly form the dough into thick disks using your palms and thumbs. Wrap the disks individually in plastic wrap. Refrigerate for 1 hour to 3 days before rolling.

RECIPE FOR A PIE & WHISKEY READING

When we started Pie & Whiskey, all we really wanted to do was make sure it was a good reading with great performances and that no one fell asleep. Which can happen at literary readings. But not at Pie & Whiskey. Sugar and booze make the reading a party and give the writers something to play with. The other important trick is to get great writers who are also great readers and make sure they write and read *short*.

But you should make the Pie & Whiskey reading your own. Use it, adapt it, remake it. The only thing that must stay the same is that there must be pie, there must be whiskey, and the readings must be short.

TO FEED AND FETE TWO TO FOUR HUNDRED, YOU'LL NEED:

- **TWENTY PIES**
  We cut the slices small; it's a loaves-and-fishes sort of situation, with everyone getting a little piece, exactly the right amount, which enhances that feeling of sharing.
- **TWENTY-FOUR FIFTHS OF WHISKEY**
  One shot free for anyone over twenty-one, extra shots available for purchase until supplies run out. The idea is to get people evenly buzzed, not drunk. They can do that after the show.

- **THIRTEEN WRITERS**
  Sometimes eleven or twelve—we say thirteen because that's a baker's dozen. More than that is too many. Less than eleven isn't enough, with everyone's reading clocking in under five minutes.
- **A VENUE THAT CAN HOLD TWO HUNDRED TO FOUR HUNDRED PEOPLE**
  Preferably an Oddfellows Hall or union bar, the older and more lived-in the better. We like a space that has some table seating and a stage for the writers.

- **MICROPHONE AND PA**
  Unless you prefer a bullhorn.
- **VOLUNTEERS TO SET UP, SERVE BOOZE, CUT PIES, AND HELP CLEAN UP**
  Even better if they have liquor and food handler's permits.
- **A LIQUOR PERMIT**

CONTINUED

1   Check your local liquor laws for the correct permit. If you have this at a bar, the bar will have the permit, and the balance of free and bought shots will probably change since that's how bars make their money.

2   Authors read in alphabetical order.

3   This reading works better if people have written new work for it. Excerpts aren't as good. We send writers a whiskey prompt and a pie prompt a few months before the event and ask them to write something new.

4   Our favorite way to throw Pie & Whiskey is to make it free, but liquor laws and practical considerations often prevent that. Compromise by keeping the door price low—three to five dollars, or seven dollars to satisfy the law and cover expenses, but no higher. Pie & Whiskey works best when people get way more than they paid for.

5   Adapt at will.

6   Pie & Whiskey is now yours.

THANK YOU

For their support of Pie & Whiskey readings, Sam and Kate would like to thank Don Poffenroth of Dry Fly Distilling, Christine Holbert of Lost Horse Press, Melissa Huggins of the Get Lit! Festival, Russ Davis at Gray Dog Press, Rosemary Small and the Spokane Woman's Club, Rachel Mindell of the Montana Book Festival, the Union Club in Missoula, and Montgomery Distillery. Kate thanks her recipe testers: Zach and Ellen Welcker, Ellen Gray, Paula Hooser, Sherrie Flick, and Margot Kahn. Chocolate Pecan Pie Whiskey Shots were invented in collaboration with Mika Maloney of Batch Bakeshop in Spokane, Washington. Thanks to the writers and participants and volunteer pie bakers, bartenders, and bouncers. Thanks to the people of Spokane and Missoula who made this what it is, the pie eaters and the whiskey drinkers who made this the best party of our lives.

ACKNOWLEDGMENTS

"The Missing and Fucking Years" © 2017 Steve Almond, first appeared in *New England Review*

"Cooking from Scratch" © 2017 Judy Blunt

"Hoh River Trail Incident" © 2017 Thom Caraway

"Blue Velvet" © 2017 Elizabeth J. Colen

"Heavenly Pies" © 2017 Anthony Doerr

"Dance" © 2017 Sherrie Flick

"Homecoming" © 2017 Jacob H. Fries

"My Youth" © 2017 Christopher Howell, first appeared in the *Gettysburg Review*

"Miles City" © 2017 Margot Kahn

"Pie and Whiskey" © 2017 Melissa Kwasny

"Chocolate Pecan Pie Whiskey Shots," "Funeral Pie," "Motherfucking Strawberry Rhubarb Pie," "My House Is Your American Gothic House," "Possibly Blueberry Pie," "Raspberry Walnut Mascarpone Hand Pies," "Three Roads to the Heart of Iowa" (first appeared in *Natural Bridge*), "Venison and Blackberry Pasties," and "Yum Yum Rum Cake" © 2017 Kate Lebo

"Dear Reader" © 2017 Kate Lebo and Samuel Ligon

"Marriage (Pie) (II)" © 2017 J. Robert Lennon

"Emma's Revelation," "John Brown's Body," "Sing a Song of Sixpence" (first appeared in *Okey-Panky*), "The Carrie Nation," "The Lonely Martha," "The Outlaw," "The Pat Nixon," "The Sacagawea Sour," "The Thirteen Wonders of Tammy" (first appeared in the *Georgia Review*), and "Whitey on the Moon" © 2017 Samuel Ligon

"Meet Me in the Bottom" © 2017 Gary Copeland Lilley

"The People Who Need It" © 2017 Robert Lopez

"Day Come White, Night Come Black" © 2017 Debra Magpie Earling

"Happy Hour" © 2017 Tod Marshall

"Straight No Chaser" © 2017 Kristen Millares Young

"And Then There Was Rum Cake" © 2017 Nina Mukerjee Furstenau

"The Captain's Delight" © 2017 Laura Read

"Bloodlines" © 2017 Virginia Reeves

"W. C. Fields Takes a Walk" © 2017 Paisley Rekdal, first appeared in *Willow Springs*

"Drinketh Thou Not the Alcohol Drink" © 2017 Nicole Sheets

"The Children's Theater" © 2017 Ed Skoog, first appeared in *Poor Claudia*

"Hunger for Pie, Dream of Whiskey" © 2017 M. L. Smoker

"Mother's Red Dress Enters a Pie in the County Fair" © 2017 Alexandra Teague, first appeared in the *Santa Clara Review*

"The Old Town" © 2017 Rachel Toor, first appeared in *American Chordata*

"I, Too, Sip from the Flask" © 2017 Nance van Winckel, first appeared in the *North American Review*

"Frito Pie" © 2017 Shawn Vestal

"Cross the Woods" (first appeared in *Esquire*) and "Whiskey Pie" © 2017 Jess Walter

"Congratulations! You Have a New Match" © 2017 Elissa Washuta

"Just a Piece of Pecan Pie (& All I Want Is You)" © 2017 Joe Wilkins

"Pie and Whiskey" © 2017 Robert Wrigley

"Story Problems" © 2017 Maya Jewell Zeller, first appeared in *Pleiades*

ABOUT THE AUTHORS

KIM ADDONIZIO's latest books are a memoir, *Bukowski in a Sundress: Confessions from a Writing Life*, and a poetry collection, *Mortal Trash*. Her story collection, *The Palace of Illusions*, was published in 2014. She is also the author of two novels and two books on writing poetry. She lives in Oakland, California, and can be found online at www.kimaddonizio.com.

STEVE ALMOND is the author of three story collections. He lives outside Boston with his wife, his children, his debt, and his anxiety.

KIM BARNES's novels have been named best books of the year by the *San Francisco Chronicle*, the *Washington Post*, and the *Kansas City Star*. She is the recipient of a PEN Center USA Literary Award as well as the PEN/Jerard Fund Award. Her first memoir, *In the Wilderness*, was nominated for a Pulitzer Prize. She teaches at the University of Idaho.

JUDY BLUNT's essay "Cooking from Scratch" was selected for the first American West Center book project, *Wo/Men at Work*, a series of handcrafted chapbooks pairing modern woman essayists with writers from the original Federal Writers' Project. Recognition for her work includes a Whiting Award, an NEA grant, and a Guggenheim Fellowship. She teaches nonfiction at the University of Montana.

THOM CARAWAY teaches at Whitworth University in Spokane, Washington, where he is also the editor of *Rock & Sling* and the publisher of Sage Hill Press. The many places he has been lost include Glacier National Park, the Frank Church–River of No Return Wilderness, Mount Spokane, the Mill Creek Watershed, and Olympic National Park. His work appears in *Redivider*, *Smartish Pace*, *Sugar House Review*, and other publications.

ELIZABETH J. COLEN's recent books include the long poem–lyric essay hybrid *The Green Condition* and the novel in prose poems *What Weaponry*. She teaches at Western Washington University.

ANTHONY DOERR's most recent novel, *All the Light We Cannot See*, won the Pulitzer Prize for Fiction and the Andrew Carnegie Medal for Excellence in Fiction and was a number-one *New York Times* best seller. He lives with his family in Boise, Idaho.

SHERRIE FLICK is the author of the novel *Reconsidering Happiness* and the short-story collection *Whiskey, Etc.* Her food essays have appeared in the *Wall Street Journal*, *Ploughshares*, the *Pittsburgh Post-Gazette*, and other publications. She writes, gardens, bakes, cooks, and drinks in Pittsburgh, Pennsylvania.

JACOB H. FRIES is the editor of the *Inlander*, a weekly newspaper covering Eastern Washington and North Idaho. His journalism has also appeared in numerous publications, including the *New York Times*, the *Boston Globe*, the *San Francisco Chronicle*, and the *Week*. He lives in Spokane with his wife, Michelle, his daughter, Julia, and their Airedale, Angus.

CHRISTOPHER HOWELL has published eleven collections of poems, most recently *Love's Last Number*, *Gaze*, and *Dreamless and Possible: Poems New and Selected*. He teaches in the MFA program at Eastern Washington University's Inland Northwest Center for Writers, in Spokane.

MARGOT KAHN is the author of *Horses That Buck*, winner of the High Plains Book Award. Her essays and reviews have appeared in *Tablet Magazine*, *River Teeth*, and the *Los Angeles Review*, among other places. She holds an MFA from Columbia University and is co-editor (with Kelly McMasters) of *This Is the Place*, an anthology of women writing about home.

MELISSA KWASNY is the author of five books of poetry, most recently *Pictograph* and *The Nine Senses*, and a collection of essays, *Earth Recitals: Essays on Image & Vision*. She edited *Toward the Open Field: Poets on the Art of Poetry 1800–1950* and coedited an anthology of poetry in defense of human rights, *I Go to the Ruined Place*.

J. ROBERT LENNON is the author of two story collections, *Pieces for the Left Hand* and *See You in Paradise*, and eight novels, including *Mailman*, *Familiar*, and *Broken River*, out in 2017 from Graywolf Press. He lives in Ithaca, New York, where he teaches writing at Cornell University.

GARY COPELAND LILLEY was a submarine sailor who spent some time under the ice. Since then he has earned an MFA from the Warren Wilson College MFA Program for Writers; facilitated over twelve thousand hours of relief work following Katrina; and had numerous works published, including four poetry collections. He sings and plays the blues. He is a Cave Canem fellow.

TOD MARSHALL was born in Buffalo, New York, grew up in Kansas, and now lives in Spokane, Washington, where he teaches at Gonzaga University. He is the author of three collections of poetry, most recently *Bugle*.

DEBRA MAGPIE EARLING is the author of *Perma Red* and *The Lost Journals of Sacajewea*. She is currently the director of the creative writing program at the University of Montana.

NINA MUKERJEE FURSTENAU has developed a passion for how cultures entwine over food through Peace Corps and lifelong travels. She has written two books, *Biting through the Skin: An Indian Kitchen in America's Heartland* and *Savor Missouri*, as well as numerous essays and articles, and she received a Kansas Notable Book award, the M. F. K. Fisher Award, and Les Dames d'Escoffier International's Grand Prize for Excellence in Culinary Writing.

LAURA READ has published poems in a variety of journals, most recently in *Rock & Sling* and *Crab Creek Review*. Her chapbook, *The Chewbacca on Hollywood Boulevard Reminds Me of You*, was the 2010 winner of the Floating Bridge Press Chapbook Award, and her collection, *Instructions for My Mother's Funeral*, was the 2011 winner of the AWP Donald Hall Prize for Poetry and was published in 2012 by the University of Pittsburgh Press. Her second collection, *Dresses from the Old Country*, will be published by BOA in fall of 2018. She teaches English at Spokane Falls Community College and currently serves as the poet laureate of Spokane, Washington.

VIRGINIA REEVES is a graduate of the Michener Center for Writers at the University of Texas at Austin. Her debut novel, *Work Like Any Other,* was long-listed for the Man Booker Prize and the Center for Fiction's First Novel Prize, and *Booklist* named it one of the top ten first novels of 2016. She lives in Helena, Montana, with her husband, two daughters, and three-legged pit bull.

PAISLEY REKDAL is the author of a book of essays, *The Night My Mother Met Bruce Lee*; a hybrid-genre photo-text memoir entitled

Intimate; and five books of poetry—most recently *Animal Eye*, which was the winner of the UNT Rilke Prize, and *Imaginary Vessels*, her newest collection. She has received the Amy Lowell Poetry Travelling Scholarship, a Guggenheim Fellowship, an NEA Fellowship, two Pushcart Prizes, a Fulbright Scholarship, and various state arts council awards. She teaches at the University of Utah.

ED SKOOG is the author of *Mister Skylight*, *Rough Day*, and *Run the Red Lights*, all published by Copper Canyon Press. His poems have appeared in *Harper's*, the *New York Times*, Best American Poetry, the *Paris Review*, *American Poetry Review*, and other publications. He is poetry editor of *Okey-Panky* and cohost, with novelist J. Robert Lennon, of the podcast *Lunch Box with Ed and John*.

NICOLE SHEETS lives in Spokane, Washington, and tweets at @heynicolesheets. She edits *How to Pack for Church Camp*, an online anthology of creative nonfiction about summer camp. Her work has appeared in *Image*, *Hotel Amerika*, *Literature and Belief*, and other publications. Her preferred pie is apple, and her preferred whiskey is whatever's in the hospitality cabinet.

M. L. SMOKER belongs to the Assiniboine and Sioux tribes of the Fort Peck Reservation in northeastern Montana. She holds an MFA from the University of Montana in Missoula, where she was the recipient of the Richard Hugo Memorial Scholarship. Her first collection of poems, *Another Attempt at Rescue*, was published by Hanging Loose Press in the spring of 2005. In 2009 she coedited an anthology of human rights poetry with Melissa Kwasny entitled *I Go to the Ruined Place*. She has also won a regional Emmy Award for her work as a writer and consultant on the PBS documentary *Indian Relay*. M. L. Smoker currently resides in Helena, Montana, where she works for the Office of Public Instruction as the director of Indian education.

ALEXANDRA TEAGUE is the author of two poetry books—*The Wise and Foolish Builders* and *Mortal Geography*—and a novel, *The Principles Behind Flotation*. A former NEA fellow and recipient of the California Book Award, she is an associate professor at the University of Idaho.

RACHEL TOOR is the author of four works of nonfiction and one novel. Her work has appeared in a variety of publications, and she writes a monthly column for the *Chronicle of Higher Education*. She graduated from Yale University and received an MFA from the University of Montana. She teaches at Eastern Washington University and lives in Spokane, Washington, with her mutt, Helen.

NANCE VAN WINCKEL's newest books are *Ever Yrs*, a novel in scrapbook form, and *Book of No Ledge*, a poetically altered encyclopedia. Nance lives in Spokane, Washington, is a professor emerita at Eastern Washington University, and teaches in Vermont College of Fine Arts' low-residency MFA in Writing program.

SHAWN VESTAL is the author of the novel *Daredevils* and *Godforsaken Idaho*, a collection of short stories. He writes a twice-weekly column for the *Spokesman-Review* in Spokane, Washington, and he enjoys all kinds of pie, even Frito pie.

JESS WALTER is the author of eight books, most recently the number-one best-selling novel *Beautiful Ruins* and the story collection *We Live in Water*. He was a finalist for the National Book Award for *The Zero* and won the Edgar Allan Poe Award for *Citizen Vince*. He lives in Spokane, Washington, with his family. His favorite pie is whiskey pecan.

ELISSA WASHUTA is a member of the Cowlitz Indian Tribe and the author of two books, *Starvation Mode* and *My Body Is a Book of Rules*, which was named a finalist for the Washington State Book Award. She is an assistant professor of English at the Ohio State University.

JOE WILKINS is the author of a memoir, *The Mountain and the Fathers: Growing Up on the Big Dry*, and three books of poetry, *When We Were Birds*, *Notes from the Journey Westward*, and *Killing the Murnion Dogs*. Wilkins lives with his family in Western Oregon, where he teaches writing at Linfield College.

ROBERT WRIGLEY is University Distinguished Professor Emeritus at the University of Idaho. He is the author of twelve books of poems, the most recent of which is *Box*. Scotch, bourbon, and rye. Huckleberry, apple, and raisin. In those orders.

KRISTEN MILLARES YOUNG is a writer and journalist whose work has been featured by the *Guardian*, the *New York Times*, KUOW, *City Arts* magazine, and *Pacifica Literary Review*. Recognized by the Society for Features Journalism, Kristen was a researcher for the Pulitzer Prize–winning *New York Times* team that produced "Snow Fall." Kristen graduated from Harvard and the MFA program at the University of Washington.

MAYA JEWELL ZELLER's books are *Rust Fish* and *Yesterday, the Bees*; her essays and poems appear widely. Maya serves as fiction editor for *Crab Creek Review* and as poetry editor for Scablands Books. Former resident in the H. J. Andrews Experimental Forest, as well as recipient of a Promise Award from the Sustainable Arts Foundation, Maya teaches creative writing at Central Washington University.

ABOUT THE EDITORS

KATE LEBO is the author of *Pie School* and *A Commonplace Book of Pie*, and she cohosts Pie & Whiskey, a reading series, with Samuel Ligon. Her work has appeared in the Best American Essays series, the Best New Poets series, *New England Review*, *Willow Springs*, and *Gastronomica*. She lives in Spokane, Washington.

SAMUEL LIGON is the author of two novels—*Among the Dead and Dreaming* and *Safe in Heaven Dead*—and two collections of stories—*Wonderland*, illustrated by Stephen Knezovich, and *Drift and Swerve*. He edits the journal *Willow Springs*, teaches at Eastern Washington University in Spokane, cohosts Pie & Whiskey with Kate Lebo, and is artistic director of the Port Townsend Writers' Conference.